T

GRAND UNION CANAL WALK

THE GRAND UNION CANAL WALK

Anthony Burton and Neil Curtis

Photographs by Derek Pratt

AURUM PRESS
in association with
British Waterways

First published by Aurum Press Ltd in association with British Waterways.

A catalogue record for this book is available from the British Library.

ISBN 1 85410 244 3

2 4 6 8 10 9 7 5 3 1

1994 1996 1997 1995 1993

Design by Robert Updegraff

Cover photograph: *Horton Lock*
Title page photograph: *Uxbridge lock.*

Printed and bound in Spain by Grafos SA, Barcelona

ACKNOWLEDGEMENTS

Our thanks go to the following. To Pip Burton for her great efforts in compiling Part 3, Useful Information. To Sheila Dallas for her logistical support while Neil Curtis was walking his sections of the Canal. To Bruce Harding, Recreation Manager for British Waterways, for all his help; to Jonathan Briggs, Conservation Officer, Environmental and Scientific Services, British Waterways, for his assistance with the feature on Wildlife and the Tring Reservoirs; J W Ellis, Fisheries Manager (South) for British Waterways for his contribution on angling; and to Mike Rumbold, Chairman, Weedon History Society for his contribution on Weedon Depot.

Contents

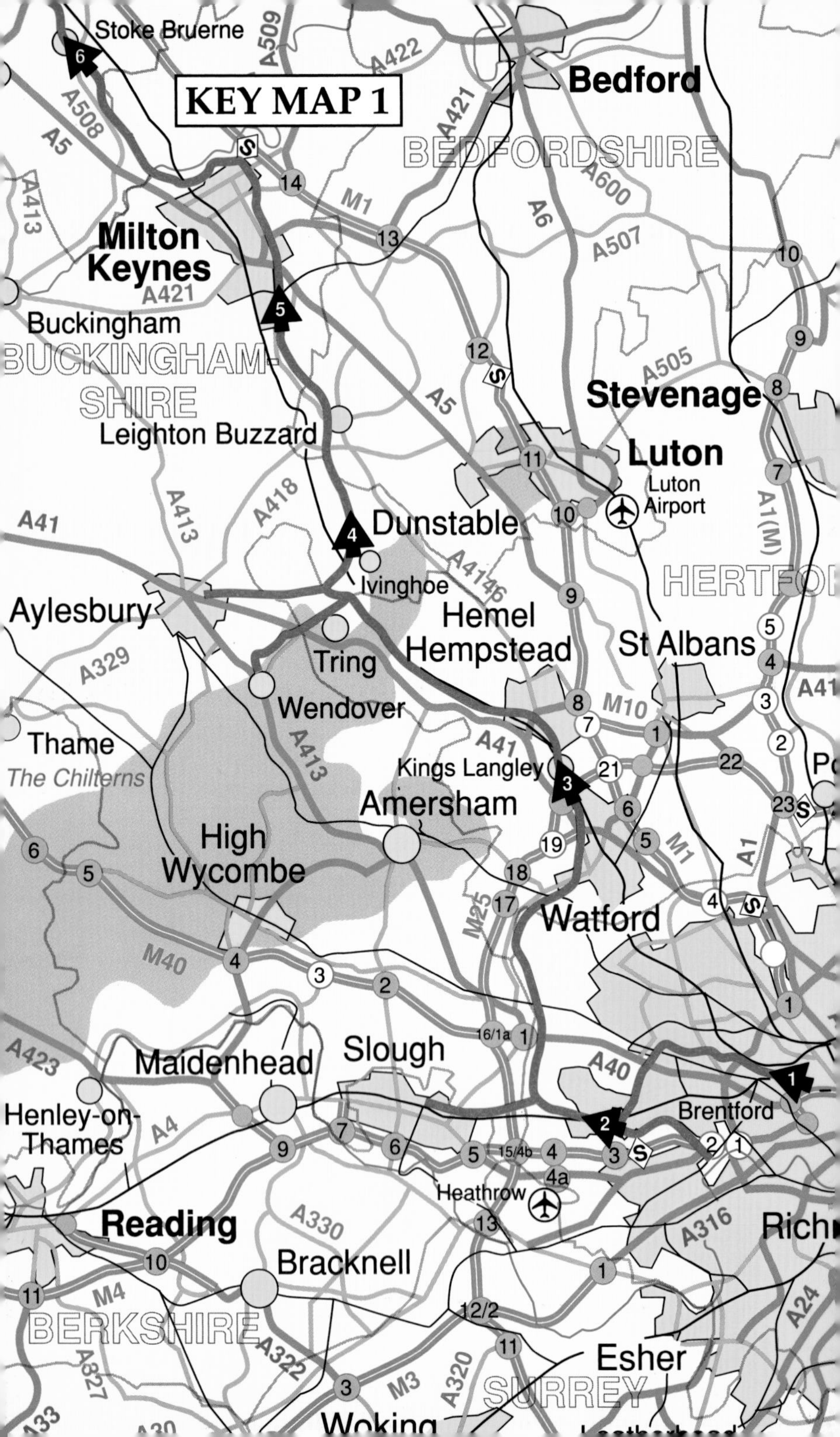

KEY MAP 1
Stoke Bruerne
Bedford
BEDFORDSHIRE
Milton Keynes
Buckingham
BUCKINGHAM-SHIRE
Leighton Buzzard
Stevenage
Luton
Luton Airport
Dunstable
Ivinghoe
HERTFO
Aylesbury
Hemel Hempstead
St Albans
Tring
Wendover
Thame
The Chilterns
Kings Langley
Amersham
High Wycombe
Watford
Slough
Maidenhead
Henley-on-Thames
Brentford
Heathrow
Reading
Bracknell
Rich
BERKSHIRE
Esher
SURREY
Woking
A509
A422
A508
A5
A413
A421
A600
A6
A507
M1
A505
A1(M)
A418
A41
A4146
A329
M10
A413
M25
M40
A423
A40
A4
A330
A316
M4
A322
A327
M3
A320
A24
A1

KEY MAPS INDEX
KEY MAP 2
KEY MAP 1
Shrewsbury
Newtown
Aberystwyth
BIRMINGHAM
Northampton
Cambridge
Lowestoft
Ipswich
Colchester
Milton Keynes
Chelmsford
Carmarthen
Monmouth
Swansea
Oxford
LONDON
CARDIFF
Swindon
Bristol
Newbury
Bath
Salisbury
Winchester
Taunton
Southampton
Dover
Folkestone
Exeter
Bournemouth
Portsmouth
Brighton
Eastbourne
Dorchester
Haverhill
Harlow
Hertford
ESSEX
Witham
Chelmsford
Maldon
Brentwood
LONDON
Ilford
Dagenham
Basildon
Tilbury
Dartford
Gravesend
Rochester
Chatham
Orpington
Croydon
KEY MAPS
Grand Union Canal
Chapter start point
0 Km 5 10 15
0 Miles 5 10

KEY MAP 2
Rugeley
Ashby-de-la-Zouch
Cannock
Lichfield
Tamworth
Wolverhampton
Walsall
Nuneaton
Dudley
BIRMINGHAM
Coventry
Bromsgrove
Redditch
Warwick
Stratford-upon-Avon
Worcester
WARWICKSHIRE
Evesham
Tewkesbury
GLOUCESTERSHIRE
Stow-on-the-Wold
Chipping Norton
The Cotswolds
A5
A5190
A449
M54
A444
A461
M42
A454
A38
M6
A446
A458
A45
A442
M5
A448
A46
A41
M40
A422
A435
A44
A4104
A429
A3400

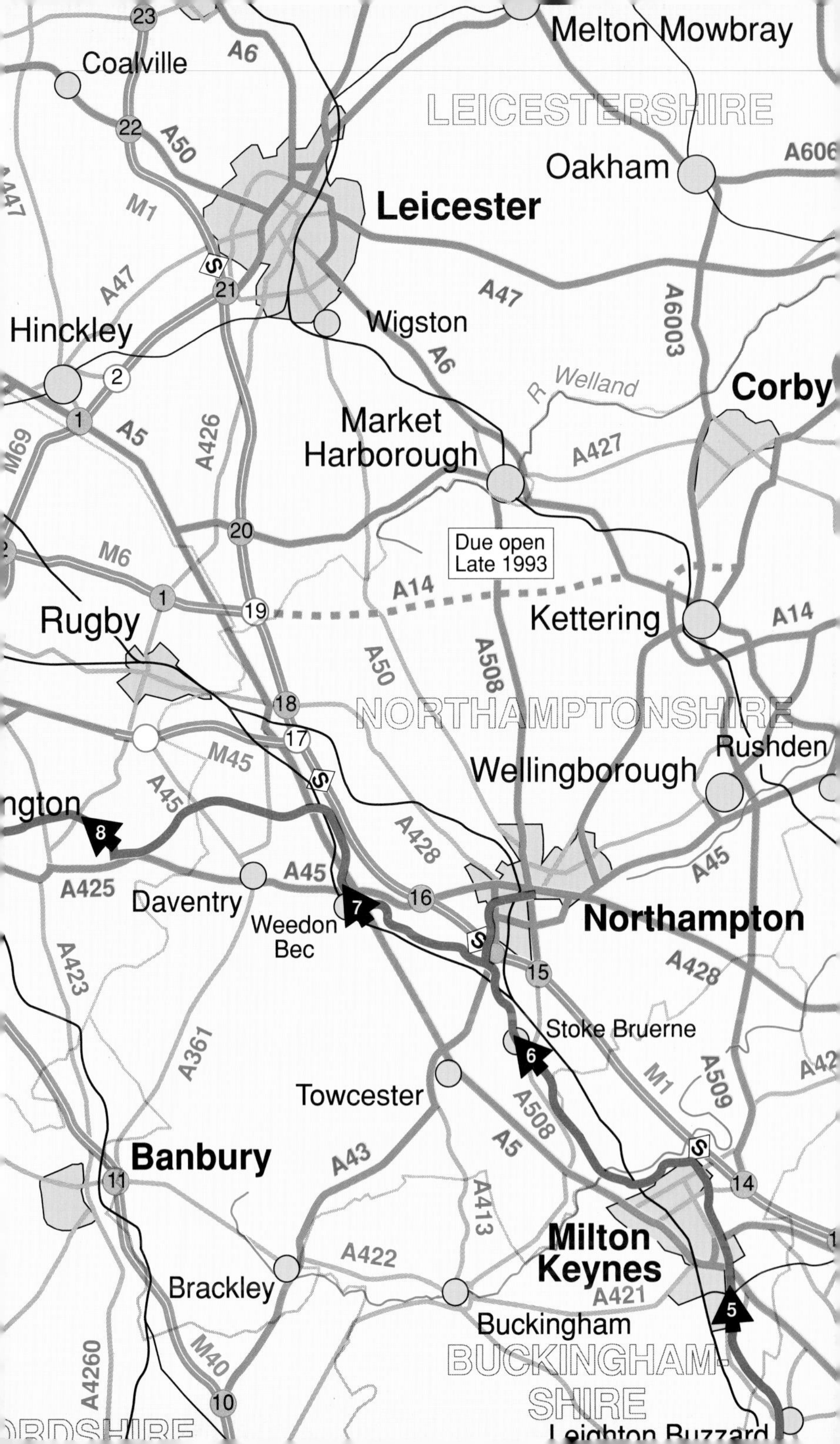
Melton Mowbray
Coalville
LEICESTERSHIRE
Oakham
Leicester
Wigston
Hinckley
R. Welland
Corby
Market Harborough
Due open
Late 1993
Kettering
Rugby
NORTHAMPTONSHIRE
Rushden
Wellingborough
Daventry
Weedon Bec
Northampton
Stoke Bruerne
Towcester
Banbury
Milton Keynes
Brackley
Buckingham
BUCKINGHAM-
SHIRE
Leighton Buzzard
A6
A50
M1
A47
A606
A6003
A5
A426
M69
A427
M6
A14
A508
A45
M45
A428
A425
A423
A361
A43
A413
A422
A421
A509
M40
A4260

How to Use This Guide

This guide to the 145½-mile (234 km) long Grand Union Canal and its branches is in three parts:

The Introduction, which gives the history of the canal and practical advice for walkers.

The path itself, split into 9 chapters, with maps opposite the description for each route section. Distances are given for each section, as well as a note of bridge numbers – which provide useful progress checks along the way. Details of the branches – to Brentford, Slough, Wendover, Aylesbury and Northampton – are given after the description of the section of the main walk where they branch off. This part of the guide contains information on places of interest along the way as well as a number of short circular walks which can be taken from different parts of the canal.

The last part includes useful information, such as local transport, accommodation and useful addresses including British Waterways local offices.

The maps have been prepared by the Ordnance Survey for this guide using 1: 50,000 Landranger maps as a base, except for the circular walks which are based on 1: 25,000 Pathfinder maps. The line of the path is shown as a dotted line, which would normally be the canal towpath, but which also includes paths over tunnels and one suggested diversion to by-pass an unsatisfactory section of towpath.

Some maps start on a right-hand page and continue on the left-hand page – black arrows ➞ at the edge of the map indicate the start point. In general the route on the main line runs from south to north, as does the route of the Brentford arm. Other arms run from their junction with the main line.

Route finding is, in general, not a problem, but there may be occasional diversions caused by towpath repair and the like, in which case walkers should follow the diversion signs set in place by British Waterways.

DISTANCE CHECKLIST

This list will assist you in calculating the distances between places on the Grand Union Canal walk where you may be planning to stay overnight, or in checking your progress along the way:

Location	*Approx. distance from previous location*	
	miles	*km*
Paddington	0	0
Alperton	5.7	9.2
Bull's Bridge	7.3	11.8
Uxbridge	6.0	9.7
Rickmansworth	7.2	11.6
Kings Langley	7.0	11.3
Berkhamsted	6.7	10.8
Ivinghoe	10.2	16.4
Leighton Buzzard	6.0	9.7
Fenny Stratford	7.5	12.1
Wolverton	9.7	15.6
Stoke Bruerne	7.8	12.6
Blisworth	4.2	6.8
Weedon	8.0	12.9
Braunston	9.0	14.5
Napton Junction	5.5	8.9
Stockton Top Lock	3.2	5.2
Leamington	7.0	11.3
Hatton Top Lock	6.5	10.5
Kingswood Junction	5.0	8.1
Solihull	6.2	10.0
Gas St Basin	11.0	17.8
Branches		
Brentford to Bulls Bridge	5.2	8.4
Slough	5.0	8.1
Wendover	6.2	10.0
Aylesbury	6.2	10.0
Northampton	5.0	8.1

PREFACE

By a quirk of history, the Canal Age happened before engine-power revolutionized transport. Two centuries ago canal construction was man-powered and canal transport was horse-powered.

Horses needed paths to tow their canal boats. Now, when British Waterways cares for the canal network mainly for leisure pursuits, we have the immense good fortune to enjoy much of the 2,000 miles of towpath. Over seven million people use these water-side walks every year – not surprising when nearly half of Britain's population lives within five miles of a waterway.

The Grand Union Canal main line and its towpath represent 140 miles of today's national network. Built at the height of the Canal Age, it features some remarkable structures from that time as well as many more recent examples of architecture and civil engineering.

Of course it passes through some of the most beautiful countryside in southern and central England. It also has many slices of secret townscape which many would claim to be the special magic of canals. As well as their tranquility, canals can be full of life. Wildlife abounds and there are other people's leisure activities to watch like boating, fishing, and sketching.

I often walk local stretches of the Grand Union Canal during lunch hours. I find it to be an excellent antidote to the stresses and pressures of modern business life.

You are sure to enjoy a walk along the Grand Union Canal. This book will add to your enjoyment. I hope the Grand Union experience will whet your appetite to walk some of our other waterways.

David Ingman
CHAIRMAN
BRITISH WATERWAYS

Part One
Introduction

The canal attracted industry: old mills line the Wendover Arm at Tring.

History of the Grand Union Canal

The word 'Union' provides a clue to the history of this route. It began its life as a series of connected but independent canals, under various owners who only joined forces as recently as 1929 to create a single company. This was not even the first Grand Union Canal – that honour belongs to the Grand Union of 1810, which was to become a part of the new amalgamation, 'Grand' no longer and now known as the Old Union.

To unravel this story one has to go back to the last decade of the eighteenth century. Britain had just emerged from a financial depression, largely caused by the very expensive, and ultimately unsuccessful, war with the young, independent nation of America. Now industry was booming, the demand for raw materials and finished goods was expanding at a tremendous rate, and so too was the demand for efficient transport. And that, in the 1790s, meant canals. Railways still lay in the future and even the best and most modern road could not hope to compete with a well-engineered waterway. Experiments conducted at the time showed that the best a single horse could achieve on a modern Macadam road was to haul a load of two tons, but that same horse could pull fifty tons along a canal. There was simply no competition. The demand was there, the potential profits were immense and there was no shortage of investors looking for something more exciting than 'the funds', low-interest government bonds. There was such a rush to put money into canal companies that these came to be known as the years of the Canal Mania. Money was poured indiscriminately into canals that were destined never to be finished, into canals that were ill-conceived and were never to recover their costs, still less show a profit, as well as into good, sensible schemes that provided vital links between thriving industrial and commercial centres. Among the latter were the canals that would subsequently make up the Grand Union.

One of the most important schemes being promoted at this time envisaged a direct route between the rapidly growing town of Birmingham, with its industries and nearby coalfield, and the commercial heart of the country, London. There was already a waterway link in existence, but it was a tenuous one: down the Birmingham and Fazeley Canal to the Coventry, along the Coventry to the Oxford, and from the Oxford down to the Thames for the final stage. Not only is it a far from direct route – the first part, along the Birmingham and Fazeley, actually ends up heading north instead of south – but it is a remarkably tortuous one. When planning a new route, early canal engineers, led by James Brindley, favoured a technique known as 'contour cutting'. They preferred to follow the natural contours of the land around hills and valleys rather than going through them in cuttings and tunnels, or across them on banks or aqueducts. This saved money on expensive engineering works but made for a wandering, wavering line – there are places on the Oxford where the curves are so extravagant that the canal almost goes through a complete circle.

There was clearly a need for a better route, and a start was made with the Act of Parliament of 1793 that authorized the beginning of work on the Grand Junction Canal, which was to run from Braunston on the Oxford Canal to the Thames at Brentford. There were to be several branches, subsequently increased by the Acts of 1794 and 1795, of which the most important was to take the Canal to its London terminus at Paddington. That same year, another canal was begun, linking Warwick to Birmingham, which was extended in 1794 by the Warwick and Napton. These canals linked up, via a short lock-free length of the Oxford Canal between Napton and Braunston, to form what is now the main line of the Grand Union between London and Birmingham. A few of the branches – Paddington, Slough, Wendover, Aylesbury and Northampton – survive; others, such as the Buckingham, have vanished. The other main part of the Grand Union system, the line to Leicester, remains an important link in the waterways network, but does not feature in the walks described in this book.

The early canals of the English Midlands had been built with narrow locks, designed to take boats approximately seven feet (2.1 metres) wide and seventy feet (21.3 metres) long, the famous canal narrow boat. The new routes of the 1790s were altogether more ambitious. In place of the old meandering line there was a new directness; the waterways carved through the

Chilterns in a deep cutting and burrowed deep under the hills at Blisworth and Braunston. And they were built to a different scale: the locks were constructed with more generous dimensions than those of the other canals. They were just as long, but twice as wide, capable of taking broad-beamed river barges. Unfortunately the canal interests of Birmingham resisted all entreaties to allow the broad canal to march up the hill to the rapidly growing town. From their point of view it was simply a question of protecting their own trade: from the point of view of canal trade as a whole, it would put a limitation on traffic that was to be keenly felt in years to come. It was a decision that was to have a profound effect on the working life of the Grand Union. But first the line had to be built.

William Jessop, the engineer in charge of the Grand Junction's construction, faced many challenges, though the first part of the route out from London was simple enough – a steady climb along river valleys. But all the time, the great ridge of the Chilterns was coming closer. The deep cutting through which the canal is channelled is an immense achievement, built without the benefit of any mechanical diggers. Rock was ripped apart by gunpowder, but everything else was done with pick-axe and shovel and the strong arms of the men who built this navigation – the 'navigators' or, as they soon became known, the 'navvies'. Even greater problems lay ahead – the crossing of the River Ouse and the two long tunnels. The Ouse crossing was very troublesome – the first embankment crumbled to be shortly followed by the collapse of the aqueduct over the river. It all had to be rebuilt. Blisworth tunnel – 3056 yards (2794 metres) long – proved even worse. Work began in 1796, but thanks largely to poor workmanship and stop-go policy of the company, it was not completed until 1805, when the whole canal could finally be declared open.

There followed an all-too-brief period of prosperity before a cloud appeared on the horizon – a cloud of dark smoke and pallid steam. The railway age had arrived and one of the first trunk routes, begun in 1833, was the line from Birmingham to London. It was a compliment to the engineering skills of Jessop and his associates that the railway engineer, Robert Stephenson, chose a line that closely followed that of the canal; but this was little consolation to the shareholders who saw profits sliding, or to boatmen who saw trade slipping away to their rival. It was now that the decision to limit traffic in the Birmingham area to narrow boats came to be seen for what it was – a short-sighted protection of local interests. But if barges could not use the Birmingham canals, the Grand Junction locks were at least big enough to take two narrow boats side by side. But two narrow boats meant two steerers – two men with wages to earn and families to support – and low company profits inevitably translated into low wages. It was railway competition that brought what we now think of as the 'traditional' boating life into being.

Before the arrival of the railways, the life of a boatman was not very different from that of a modern long-distance lorry driver. He might be away for days at a time, but he had a home and family to return to. Now economic necessity drove such families out of their homes 'on the land' and they took up a new, nomadic life, living on the boats. It is difficult, today, to imagine bringing up a family in a space around seven feet (just over 2 metres) square, but the back cabin of a narrow boat offered no more. Here the family lived, cooked and slept in a jigsaw puzzle

Country pleasures brought to town: fishermen at Carlton Bridge on the Paddington Arm.

Traditional craft at Gas Street, Birmingham.

of pull-down tables, cupboards, beds and cross-beds. The arrival of power – steam at first, then diesel – brought the working pair, the motor boat towing the unpowered butty behind it. That at least gave the families two cabins to live in. Space may have been small, but the families set about making it homely and expressed pride in their floating homes through the famous decoration of painted roses and castles, shining brasses and fine rope-work. Many of the pubs along the Grand Union were traditional boaters' pubs where families got together not just to drink but to shop and exchange news and gossip. The canal was their world.

The canals survived the coming of the railways, but the internal combustion engine and the motor truck posed a far greater threat. It was obvious that modernization was needed. The Grand Junction had already taken over the line to Leicester in 1897, but in 1929 it joined forces with the Regent's Canal and the companies that formed the line from Napton to Birmingham to create the Grand Union. The old narrow locks north of

Braunston gave way to new broad locks and there were improvements throughout the whole canal. In 1934 they began their own carrying firm, the Grand Union Canal Carrying Company, with a large fleet of boats. It all came too late, however. The days of commercial carrying by narrow boats was coming to an end. Nationalization in 1949 brought only a temporary reprieve and trade continued to decline almost to vanishing point.

As early as 1853, a Mr Robins was writing that although traffic on the canal was reducing, 'the cheap trips into the country offered by its means during the summer months are beginning to be highly appreciated'. In 1891, a book called *Two Girls on a Barge* described how the young ladies in question adapted a working narrow boat for pleasure-cruising on the Grand Union. The transformation included hanging Liberty curtains in what had been the hold – which must have astonished 'Mr Bargee and Mrs Bargee' who came along to work the boat. Today, converted narrow boats are a commonplace on the canal; some used as camping boats have scarcely changed since their working days, others have cabins and roofs where once planks and sheets covered the hold. Alongside these are literally hundreds of new narrow boats, purpose built for pleasure boating, but still showing their origins in the traditional design of the hull.

Pleasure-boating has brought traffic back to the canals, but boaters are not the only ones who come to the canal for pleasure and relaxation. Anglers line the banks and walkers are increasingly finding the towpath to be a ready-made long-distance footpath. It provides an ideal route through country and town, but always has the added fascination of being part of a transport system that two centuries ago was the most important route of the day – the M1 of the eighteenth century.

PRACTICAL ADVICE

Towpath walking is ideal for those who are not keen on hill-climbing. It is in the nature of canals that they remain on the level and only go up and down in gentle stages through single locks, or locks grouped together to form a flight. The greatest leap on the Grand Union, the 21 locks at Hatton, have a rise of rather less than 150 feet (46 metres) and are spread out over nearly two miles, so that they can scarcely be called challenging to the walker passing alongside them – certainly a good deal less challenging than they are for the boater with 84 heavy lock gates to open and close and 84 sets of paddle gear to wind up and down. Having said that, however, the London to Birmingham walk is a long one and the towpath is narrow – and narrower and less even than it was in the days when horses regularly tramped this way hauling the boats. Ordinary shoes may be adequate for a short stroll, but for a longer walk proper walking shoes or even boots will prove far more comfortable. Some sections of the towpath are in less than perfect condition. The authors have tried to indicate these places in the text, but circumstances change: some sections will no doubt be improved, but, being by the water, another section can easily crumble and be washed away. The path is generally narrow – single file walking is very much the order of the day.

The usual precautions for long-distance walking should be taken. You can get just as wet caught in a storm over the Canal as you can in a downpour on the Pennine Way, so good wet-weather gear is essential, especially for those following the whole route. A simple first-aid kit – including plasters for blisters – is always worth taking. In general, shops and pubs turn up at fairly frequent intervals but, as the authors can testify, you always seem to get thirstiest when you are furthest away from any facilities. There are special conditions that require special precautions. Because the path is narrow, briars, thorns and nettles cannot always be avoided and wearers of shorts may well end the day with stings and scratches. Sadly, in urban areas, there is always the chance of meeting some fairly unsavoury characters – something of which solitary walkers, particularly women, should be aware. In general, though, the route offers delightful, very easy and undemanding walking in both town and country.

WILLIAM JESSOP *(1745–1814)*

William Jessop was chief engineer for the Grand Junction Canal, yet his name is not well known today, except among a small number of canal enthusiasts. In part this was due to his personal modesty – a great contrast to his famous contemporary, the enthusiastic self-publicizer, Thomas Telford. Yet his achievements were great and his was the guiding hand that led many a scheme through to a successful conclusion in the turbulent years of the Canal Mania of the 1790s.

William Jessop's father was a foreman shipwright whose first encounter with civil engineering came when he was given responsibility for maintenance of the Eddystone Lighthouse off Plymouth. It was destroyed in a gale in 1755 and the task of building a replacement went to one of the great engineers of the day, John Smeaton. The gale was a piece of good fortune for young William for he was apprenticed to Smeaton at the age of fourteen, and so began probably the best engineering apprentice-

The tall tower stands above a ventilation shaft at Blisworth tunnel.

ship available at that time. He went on to work with Smeaton until 1772, becoming involved in major inland waterway projects, including the Calder and Hebble Navigation and the Forth and Clyde Canal. By 1772 he felt sufficiently confident to set up in business on his own and steadily built up a reputation as a thoroughly sound and trustworthy engineer.

When the great rush of plans for new canals began to appear in the 1790s, Jessop was in the ideal position at the ideal time. He had maturity and experience, but was still young enough to be full of vigour and receptive to new ideas. There was scarcely a canal scheme in the 1790s in which he was not involved, some of them offering the greatest challenges of the day. He was responsible for the Rochdale Canal which was blasted and driven through the Pennine Hills and for the Ellesmere, now better known as the Llangollen, with its mighty aqueduct of Pont Cysyllte. It was on the Ellesmere that Telford was given his first canal engineering job under Jessop's command, and credit for the majestic work lies with them both. In many ways, the Grand Junction was the greatest of them all, and shows Jessop using every conceivable technique to provide the best and most efficient route from London towards Birmingham – at times snaking round obstacles, in other places striding over valleys on high banks and tall aqueducts, elsewhere burrowing deep underground.

It was not only as a canal engineer that Jessop achieved his success. He was one of the pioneers of railway construction and his work included the world's first independent public railway, the Surrey Iron Railway, opened in 1803 – but using horses, not steam, for haulage. He did important, if unromantic work, on land drainage and was one of the foremost designers of docks of his day. His work included West India Docks in London and the Bristol Floating Harbour. William Jessop could truly be called the complete engineer.

THE GRAND CANAL

The Grand Junction Canal in England was opened in March 1805 – and two months later another Grand Canal was opened, not from London to Birmingham, but from Dublin to the Shannon. The Irish canal had, however, been a lot longer in the making.

It was begun, in a mood of high optimism, in 1756 by the Commissioners of Inland Navigation and it was designed to a massive scale, with 136-foot-long (41-metre) locks able to take

175-ton barges. The early optimism soon faded. By 1770 only twenty miles of canal had been built – and none of that completed to a condition where it could be used by boats – while £70,000 had been spent. In 1772 the Commissioners decided that enough public money had been used, and the whole scheme was passed over to a private company. One of their first actions was to call in an expert from England, John Smeaton, and here the connection was established that was to link the two Grand Canals, for Smeaton brought with him his young assistant, William Jessop, who was to remain as an adviser and consultant for the project until its completion. One of the first decisions that Jessop took was to reduce the whole canal to a more manageable scale – the gargantuan locks were shrunk to a length of 70 feet (21 metres) and a width of 13 feet 7½ inches (4 metres) – not so very different from those of the Grand Junction. Now work proceeded at a more respectable pace, and in 1779 the first twelve-mile section was opened for traffic, though it was to be over twenty years before the whole 79 miles between Dublin and Shannon harbour could be used.

As on the Grand Junction, traffic reached a peak in the nineteenth century and gradually faded away, until, in May 1960, the last working boat ceased trading. Like the Grand Junction, the Grand Canal is now finding a new role as a route for holidaymakers, and there can be few better ways to explore the rural heartland of Ireland than on this canal. Its 36 locks – ten of them arranged in staircase pairs – are comfortably spaced, near enough together to ensure continuous interest, far enough apart so as not to become tiring. The scenery varies from the flat bogs, where peat is still cut for fuel, to peaceful wooded cuttings and parkland. The towns along the way are attractive, many with wharves and warehouses that thrived in busier times, and some with quite grand hotels, reminders of the days when passenger boats plied the Grand Canal. Like its counterpart in England, the Irish canal forms a valuable link with other waterways, particularly the two major rivers, the Barrow and Shannon.

The two waterways have had remarkably similar careers: both had William Jessop in control, both have seen commercial traffic rise and decline, both have been nationalized – and now both are being rediscovered and enjoying a new life as holiday routes. The Grand Canal and The Grand Union Canal are now officially twinned.

Part Two
The Walk

1
PADDINGTON TO BULL'S BRIDGE

13 MILES (21 KM)

The walk begins at Little Venice, by the junction of Warwick Avenue and Bloomfield Road, close to Warwick Avenue tube station. Here the canal is crossed by a handsome iron footbridge, resplendent in blue and gold and boasting the Paddington coat of arms. Take the towpath past the island, which marks the junction between the Regent's Canal, the short arm of the Grand Union that leads down to Paddington Basin, the original terminus of the Grand Junction Canal, and the main line heading off towards Birmingham. At the next bridge there is an amazing collection of urns, pillars and decorative fountains. Cross the bridge and take the towpath underneath past the old toll house, now used as offices by British Waterways. Beyond the bridge is an array of houseboats, some almost as grand as the early nineteenth-century houses that stand behind them – something of a contrast with the twentieth-century severity on the towpath side.

At this end of the Canal, the towpath is paved, and is a popular local footpath. It is an area of great contrasts. Here are the converted working narrow boats, now Jasons Trip Boats, a colony of Canada geese and, opposite, high-rise flats with a Victorian church lurking in the middle. The church, St Mary Magdalene, has an ornate tower and steeple, banded with alternating layers of brick and stone. Beyond that, contrast again, this time between modern flats and a brooding Victorian school, now an Adult Education Centre. A covered walkway links older buildings now converted to offices. Beyond Harrow Road Bridge are new flats in the fashionable style of the 80s – brick and tile, bays and balconies and a bewildering array of pitched roofs. Beyond them, two stark, white towers rise up.

The towpath now passes under the shadow of the vast concrete canopy of the Westway section of the M40, heading towards

Carlton Bridge. The *Carlton Bridge Tavern* has a small canal-side courtyard and a canal pub sign to match the more usual one by the road. This is very much an urban area, but one full of interest and contrasts. High-rise flats mix with Victorian terraces; wharves and warehouses may be neglected but, by the canal, a community association offers a boat club and canoeing facilities for local children. A modern footbridge has adopted older forms with decorative railings and ornate lanterns, while older houses have walls rising sheer from the canal and balconies that overhang it. A wall has a bright, cheery mural with a watery theme, and a gap reveals a sculpture court where Spiderman hangs in a web of chains, while across the water is the charming Harrow Road Public Library, its name carved in Roman capitals. And there is a moment of frivolity at the *Flore* pub where windows painted on the wall appear to open out to exotic tropical scenes.

The towpath crosses an old arm that leads to the now disused Porta Bella Dock, and opposite a gatehouse leads to Kensal Green Cemetery, packed with elaborate, romantic Victorian memorials **(A)**. The living are looked after at Bridge 5 where a

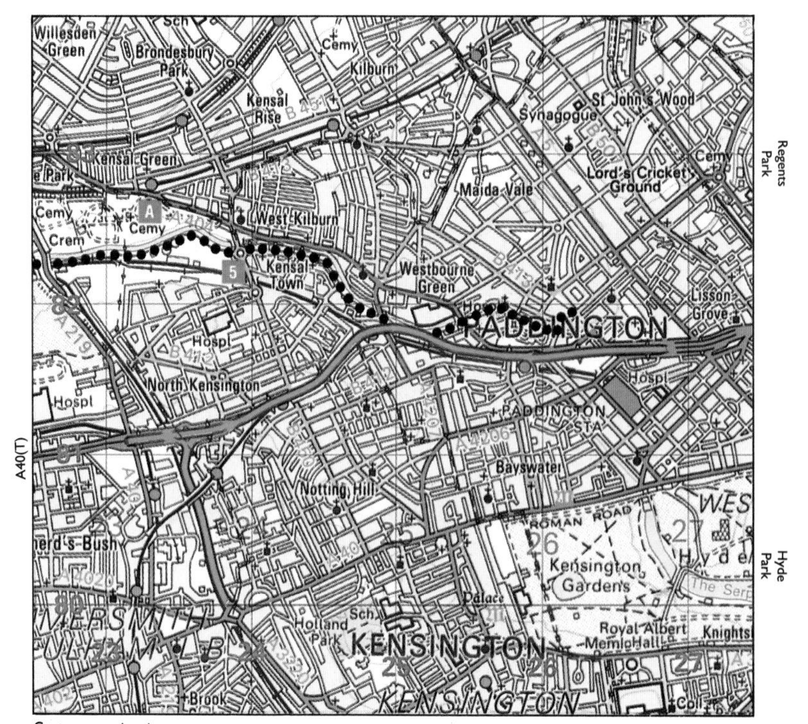

Contours are given in metres
The vertical interval is 10m

new Sainsbury's offers mooring for customers and has a coffee-shop alongside the store. Beyond it the apparently fragile, lace-like girders of gas holders rise up and short arms lead into the old gas works. There now follows a surprisingly green and peaceful section, where trees and shrubs line the canal – poplar, sycamore, chestnut and a profusion of brambles. Occasional breaks on the towpath side give a view of the extensive railway freight depot and new electrified line: the new high-tech sheds look very smart alongside the Old Oak Common Depot where 125s sulk under what are now rather old and battered covers. Beyond the colourful rail bridge and rather less dramatic Scrubs Lane road bridge, there is a view across to the dour walls of Wormwood Scrubs prison and a wide panorama of the London skyline.

There follows an area of rather nondescript industrial buildings interspersed with wasteland, but enlivened with bright patches of Michaelmas daisies. This is also a section for interesting aromas: sweet biscuity smells from McVities; more pungent from a canal-side soup company. There are constant changes of scene: a communication tower rears up, bristling with receiver dishes, then the towpath slices into rising ground through a green, shallow cutting to emerge at Harlesden amid a flurry of bridges, dominated by a rather grand brick railway bridge, built on the skew. After the modernity of the new freight depot it comes as a surprise to see an old-fashioned semaphore signal

London at its most elegant, near the start of the walk at Little Venice.

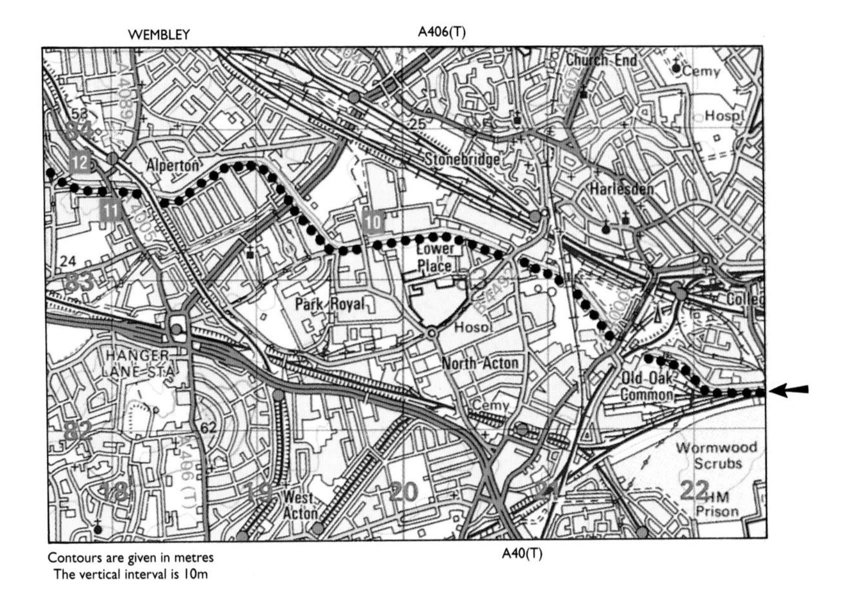

standing above the tracks. After that, the view is dominated by the gaunt concrete walls and shapely cooling towers of Acton Lane power station. Beyond it is the colourfully painted iron bridge, Number 9, and the suitably imposing *Grand Junction Arms* with a narrow boat on the sign. In among these very urban buildings is an area of allotments with a fine array of home-made sheds and greenhouses. But the strong scent of tomatoes comes not from there but from the nearby Heinz factory. It still has the wharves where boats once called, but now they are closed off behind high railings.

A new concrete road bridge, Number 10, leads to another factory area where grounds have been landscaped and planted with trees. Then there is a dramatic opening-out of the scene as the canal crosses the busy North Circular Road on a new concrete aqueduct. This marks something of a change of scene. Now more green spaces appear where willows loll elegantly over the water; the industrial area gives way to suburbia, and there are rows of neat brick boxes with equally trim gardens. The London tube trains rattle over a long multi-arched viaduct. At Alperton Bridge there is a sudden eruption of colour as a startlingly bright tower block appears in red and three shades of blue. Bridge 11 brings another pub, *The Pleasure Boat,* and another Sainsburys, this time in cosy red brick and tile. Then comes the first 'traditional' canal bridge, Number 12 – a brick arch, a string course and above that bricks laid on a curve with stone coping at the top. And here too one comes out into open country by Sudbury Golf Course. The towpath is no longer surfaced and the accompanying hedgerow is bright with hawthorn and dog roses. It is an attractive area, popular with birds – though the birds may not always be popular with the humans. A pair of Canada geese had made themselves at home in a bunker, creating a novel golfing hazard.

Where the golf course ends is an area of wilder, uncultivated land and a view across to wooded Horsenden Hill (**B**), rising up behind the houses. Soon another brick bridge, Number 13, appears, reinforced by tie beams, with the date 1909 and the canal company's initials. This is a very leafy area, with trees bowing low over the water and dense, scrubby woodland on the towpath side; Perivale Wood has, in fact, been a nature reserve since 1902. Then industry reappears in the shape of the Glaxo factory and a batch of industrial units. These are certainly not without interest; older works often have signs of former canal use in the shape of bricked-up arches while others are a mass of mysteriously squirming pipes like silvery intestines. Many factories have set out areas of greenery with walks and benches and the towpath itself has been renovated. The canal itself goes into a series of sharp bends, and is now home to craft on permanent moorings.

Western Avenue Bridge brings another area of dense scrub – complete with warning notices about pollution, which are

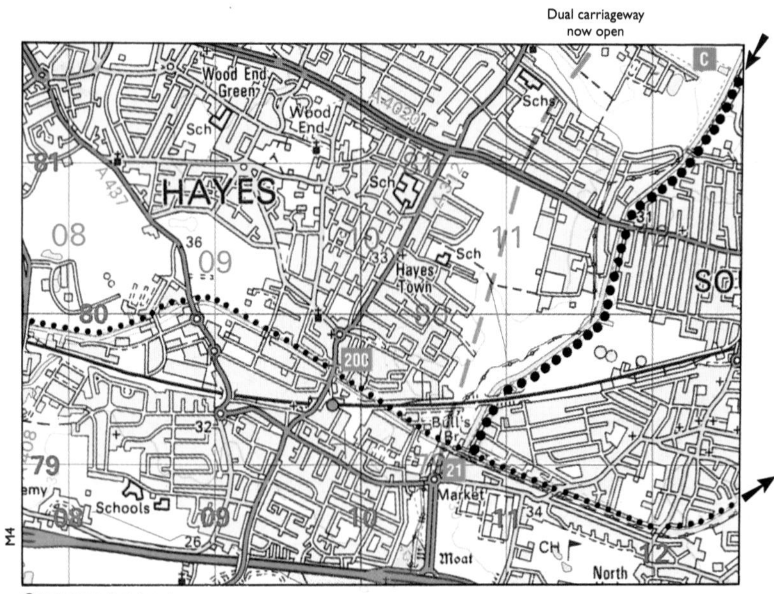

Contours are given in metres
The vertical interval is 10m

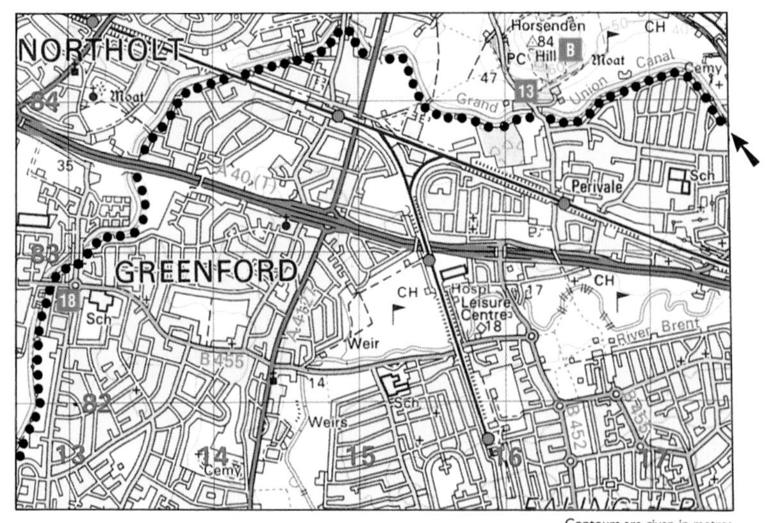

Contours are given in metres
The vertical interval is 10m

ignored by the local heron population. There are flats and houses beyond the water, but on the towpath side buildings are screened from view by trees, including some very fruitful crab apple. At Bridge 18, the Taylor Woodrow offices straddle the canal and are followed by new houses in Colditz-like isolation. It is a relief to arrive at an open area with playing fields, joined by a quite handsome concrete bridge. This is followed by a new development, West Quay Village (**C**). The houses line a newly created basin, with pontoons for mooring. Space round here seems very well used with adventure playgrounds and conventional football pitches. This ends with the houses, factories and stores of Southall, which in turn give way to an area dominated by two immense gas-holders. The actual gas works has gone, levelled to create a storage area for new cars, hidden from sight behind a high brick wall. It is, however, a very peaceful area, popular with wildfowl.

A new concrete road bridge, followed by a railway bridge and a sudden flurry of boats, announces the arrival of Bull's Bridge Junction, the end of the Paddington Arm. To the left, the original main line leads down to Brentford and the Thames; to the right the towpath heads onwards towards Birmingham. Cross Bridge 21 to join the towpath at the old toll house, with its two massive wooden rudders in the garden, and follow the towpath round to the right. Bridges are now numbered down from Braunston, so the next bridge will be Number 200.

Modern development where the Great West Road crosses the canal.

The Brentford Arm

This is not, strictly speaking, an arm at all, but the original main line of the Grand Junction Canal and could provide an alternative starting point for the route to Birmingham. The first part of the waterway makes use of the River Brent, but no longer has a continuous towpath, so the walk begins at the bridge in Brentford High Street. Join the towpath and head towards the two locks, Number 100 counting from Braunston. These are gauging locks where boats were assessed for the value of their cargo and the tolls to be paid. There is a small control cabin for the automatic locks and a handsome octagonal toll office.

Beyond the locks is a wide basin, lined with canopied warehouses, where boats could be loaded and unloaded in the dry. The towpath crosses a small swing bridge over an arm then passes right through one of the big warehouses, beneath the echoing canopy. It goes under a railway bridge and approaches a mixed area of office development along the Great West Road, the A4. To one side is the 80s style, vaguely traditional with brick and pitched roofs, while opposite is the other style of the times, low and high-tech. Beyond the bridge are the somewhat earlier and duller tower blocks. Offices have gardens and canal-side seats and a new wooden footbridge crosses the canal at Boston Manor Park. There is a countrified air here, with access to extensive parkland.

Clitheroe Lock is a typical Grand Union lock, still boasting massive wooden bollards, one of which has been almost sliced through by countless mooring ropes. Beyond that a concrete weir leads down to the river and a mass of green trees. The M4 traffic rushes past overhead, but here among the trees – willow, elder, hawthorn and oak – one can see kestrel, wagtail, fishing herons and even the occasional kingfisher. The canal is crossed by the iron Gallows Bridge, cast, like those at Braunston, by the Horseley Iron Works. It originally proclaimed itself as being 'Grand Junction Canal 1820', but the word 'Junction' has been removed and 'Union' crudely printed in. Here the towpath changes sides and enters a lovely, tree-shaded section, crossed by the multi-arched viaduct that carries the Piccadilly line. The walk now enters the area of the Brent River Park **(A)**, which stretches all the way to Western Avenue and contains areas of genuine wild countryside. Beyond the motorway is an area of dense woodland, dominated by tall oak which leads up to Osterley Lock. The Brent is crossed on a low bridge and there is a view of one of the river's botanical features – giant hogweed as much as 10 feet (3 metres) high. A plaque announces that this section won a prize for its piling in 1959. There is a contrast now between the industrial buildings interspersed with grassland on the offside and housing which reaches

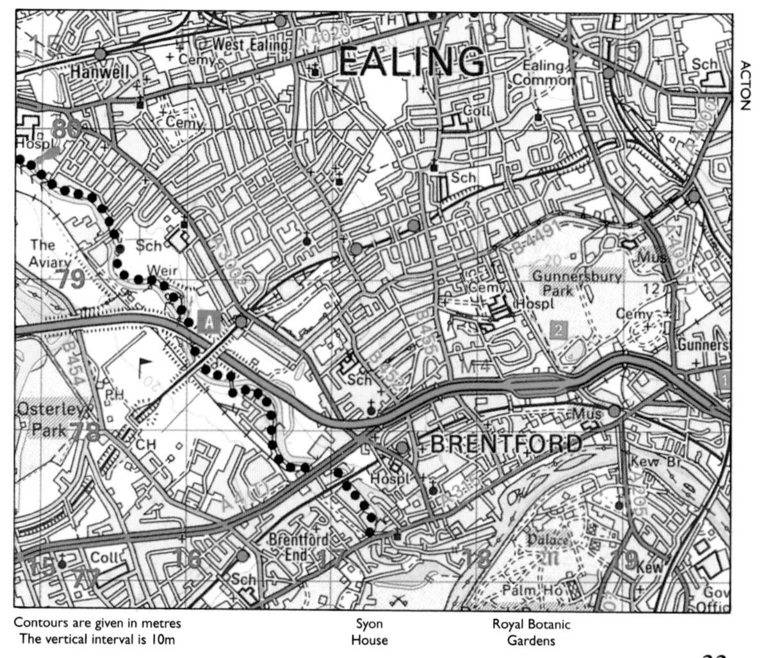

Contours are given in metres
The vertical interval is 10m

Syon House

Royal Botanic Gardens

up to the canal on the towpath side. At the foot of Hanwell Locks, the River Brent swings away to the right while the six locks climb steeply up the hill past Ealing hospital, the new building offering an amazing array of pagoda-like roofs. On the towpath side, the hospital is screened by a very decorative brick wall, half-way up which is a bricked-in archway. This once allowed boats in to deliver coal to what was then a mental hospital – hence the name of this lock, Asylum Lock. There are lock cottages at either end, the top one being particularly attractive, with round-headed windows, and features along the way include a small ramp running down into the water, which allowed any horse that accidentally fell into the canal to get out again. There are also a cast-iron distance post and bollards worn to sculptural forms.

Beyond the top lock is 'Three Bridges' **(B)** where the road runs over the canal and the canal runs over the railway – the railway also finished up on the canal in the shape of a bridge guard made out of old GWR rail. An old wharf now houses the Ealing sea cadets depot, but in general the area is built up as far as the two Norwood Locks, with their sadly derelict lock cottage. After that a high-arched bridge leads over the arm to Maypole Dock with boat moorings. This is a residential area, with many houses having long gardens running down to the water, so that it still

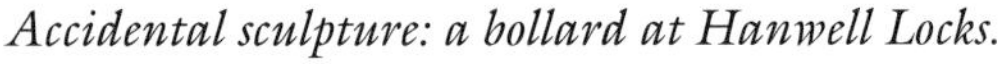

Accidental sculpture: a bollard at Hanwell Locks.

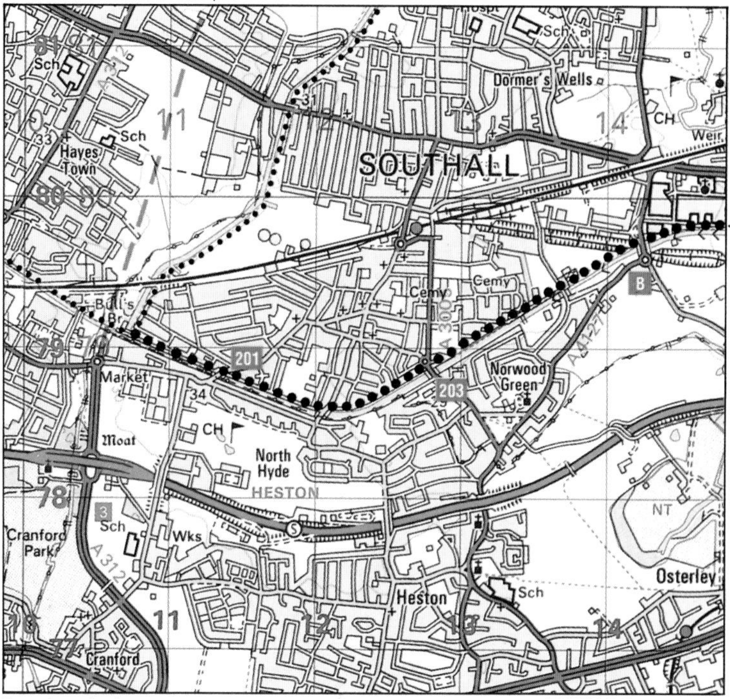
Dual carriageway
now open
SOUTHALL
Dormer's Wells
Hayes Town
Bull's Br
Market
Moat
North Hyde
HESTON
Norwood Green
Cranford Park
Cranford
Heston
Osterley
201
203
M4
Osterley Park
HOUNSLOW
Contours are given in metres
The vertical interval is 10m

seems remote – but pop up on to Bridge 203, for example, by *The Lamb* pub and you find yourself in the middle of a busy town scene. Beneath the bridge, the towpath is cobbled and leads to an old works, and beyond is Adelaide Dock, base for T & D Murrell, many of whose barges can be seen along the canal. Other short arms and wharves once served a multiplicity of works, including a private arm down to the Quaker Oats factory.

There is a somewhat run-down area, where rubbish spills on to the canal bank – but it seems not to have affected the mallard and moorhen that crowd the water. In among the modern houses is a curiously named Victorian pair – Industrious Cottages. Thirsty walkers are well provided for with *The Old Oak Tree* at Bridge 202 followed by *The Grand Junction Arms* at 201. In among a mass of new industrial building is a colony of houseboats – some conventional, some caravans on pontoons and some looking like suburban houses that have been cast adrift. This section of the canal ends at Bulls Bridge – once home to a huge fleet of Grand Union narrow boats, and now being developed as the site for a supermarket. To the right lies the Paddington Arm.

A misty morning walk by the River Brent at Hanwell.

A Circular Walk from Hanwell Bottom Lock

2 ¼ miles (3.6 km)

The walk starts by the top gates of Hanwell Bottom Lock. Turn right on to the footpath signposted 'Fitzherbert Walk' which runs along beside the River Brent. Follow the path down to pass under the road bridge with the ornamental balustrade. At the far side of the bridge, climb up the steps and continue to follow the path along the river bank towards the railway viaduct. At the viaduct cross the river on the small footbridge and turn left to enter the park beyond the viaduct. Turn left on the path and continue following the line of the river, passing the lefthand side of the bowling green. Continue along the river to a set of wooden steps on the bank. Go down the steps and cross the river on the footbridge.

Turn right on the far side of the bridge, past the cricket field. The path rejoins the river by the golf course. Follow the river and cross at the second footbridge at the edge of the golf course. Turn left, then immediately right on to the footpath. At the road, turn right to join the pedestrian way that leads straight into a footpath screened by trees. The path climbs steeply uphill and emerges in a suburban street. Turn right to walk past the small thatched cottage towards the church. Immediately before the church turn left on to the avenue bounded by horse chestnuts, which leads through the park. At the road turn right to pass under the viaduct into Station Road. Continue on to the main road, turn right and cross the road at the traffic lights by *The Viaduct* pub. Turn left into Lower Boston Road and right into Green Lane next to the school. Follow Green Lane back down to the canal.

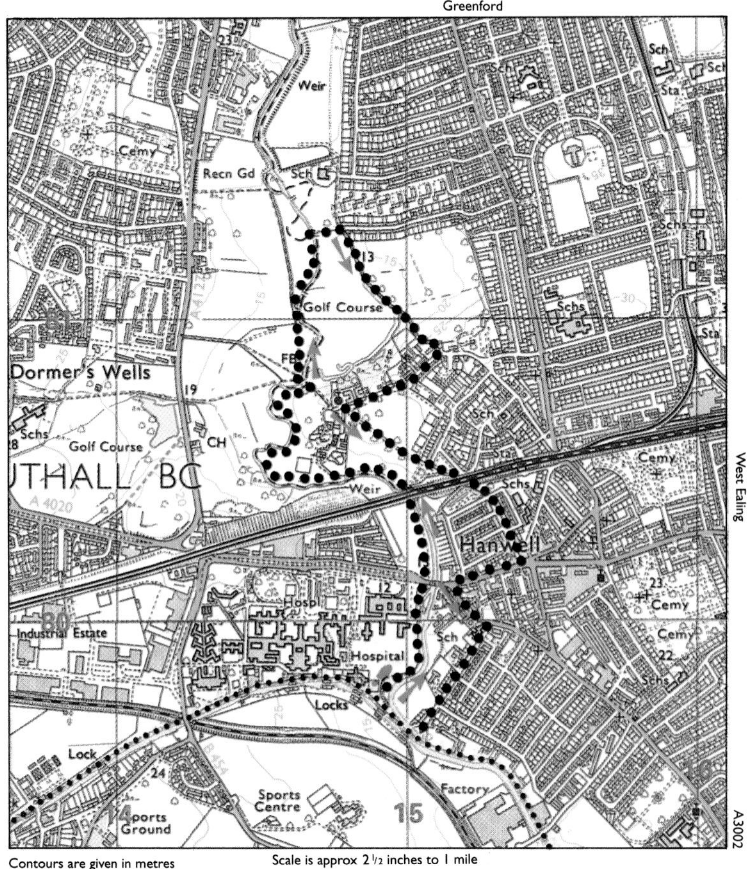

Contours are given in metres
The vertical interval is 5m

Scale is approx 2 ½ inches to 1 mile

2
BULL'S BRIDGE TO KING'S LANGLEY

20 1/4 MILES (32.6 KM)

The canal crosses a tree-shaded brook on a short aqueduct before plunging into the industrial area of Hayes. The bypass sweeps overhead on concrete pillars, but between the electricity sub-station and the giant Nestlé factory is one small field where cows stolidly munch. The mainline railway bridge shows signs of extensive widening over the years and a prospect of tower blocks announces the arrival of the town centre. A sadly dilapidated brick bridge, scheduled for repair, now carries the towpath across an abandoned arm. This is not a very attractive area, but the canal itself provides a green corridor and a busy wildlife habitat – a peacock butterfly was enjoying a meal of blackberry.

Bridge 199, with an attractive new number plate, marks something of a boundary – an end to some of the heavily industrialized areas and the beginning of the rapidly developing new. The more recent developments show a welcome awareness of the canal, with gardens and benches overlooking the water. Bridge 198 is an unusual road bridge, with the arch lined in blue engineering brick. All along the canal there are reminders of the old days of factories served by boat, in the shape of wharves and mooring rings, but they are overwhelmed by the spread of modern units, mainly low-rise, but covering an immense area of land. Rather sadly, many of the attractively landscaped grounds can only be seen through high chain-link fences. At Bridge 195, the bricks that form the towpath are each and every one inscribed '1912' while the bricks in the bridge are '1914'. The next industrial unit actually has stiles to give access between towpath and grounds and has set its security fence further back – a happier solution due to be extended to the other sites. Where there are no new buildings, the canal is already being prepared for them.

The elegant junction bridge at Bull's Bridge.

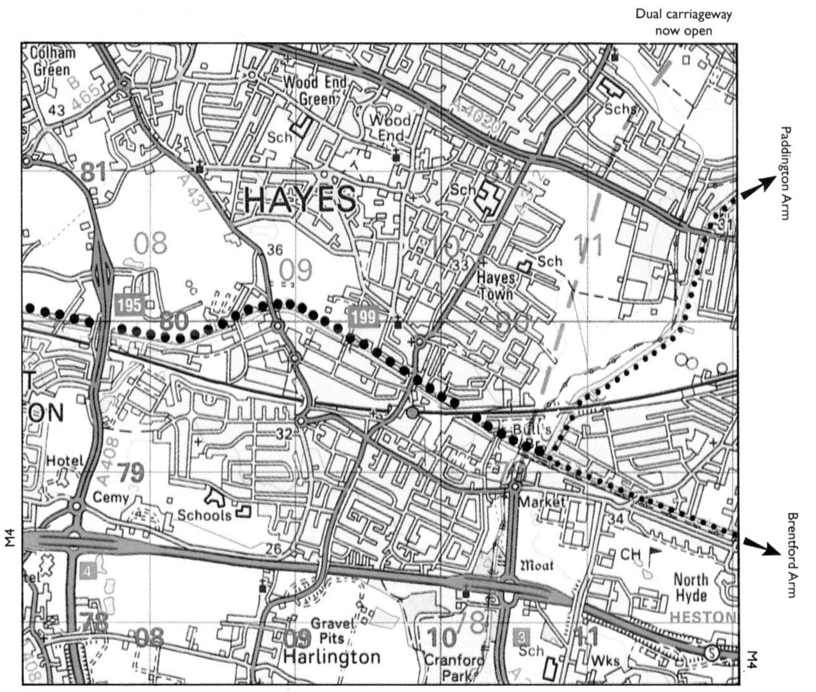

Contours are given in metres
The vertical interval is 10m

Opposite the rather attractive, countrified station of West Drayton **(A)** is a new housing estate which looks back to older vernacular forms – one house has a patterned, tile-hung gable wall. In among the houses and factories a kingfisher kept us company, dashing out from the trees and darting for cover in more shrubs before reappearing up ahead. Across the water, houses have balconies jutting out over the canal and their own canal-side walkway.

On the towpath side are a number of older industrial buildings, including one with a 'waggon corner', rounded to allow carts to slip by without knocking the brickwork about. Bridge 191 is dotted with iron tie-beams, still carrying the Grand Junction Canal Company name. After that it comes as a not unpleasant surprise to come across an area of fields and grazing cows. This is Cowley Peachey Junction where the Slough Arm runs off to the left **(B)**. From here, in 1801, passengers could get the Paddington Packet all the way to Paddington Basin – a journey that took the best part of a day at the pace of an ambling horse.

The area around the junction is crammed with moored craft, including a number of old working boats, now converted for holiday use. An equally successful conversion has turned an old wharf building by Bridge 190 into the *Turning Point* restaurant. Although this is still a built-up area, the green fringe gives the towpath a comfortable, countrified air and this is helped by the appearance of a traditional hump-backed bridge, Number 189. The approach to Cowley Peachey lock is particularly pleasant: trees drape branches over the path and at the lock itself is a pair of lock cottages built against the bank so that there are roadside entrances at ground-floor level and separate entrances, at lock-level, to the first floor. Beyond that is a short aqueduct, *The Jolly Anglers* and, almost buried in tarmac, an old canal mile-post announcing that there are 83 miles still to go to Braunston.

The path crosses Bridge 188 and continues on the opposite bank of the canal. The rural interlude ends with the approach to Uxbridge. A skeletal gas-holder contrasts with new high-rise blocks and, beyond them, a new Uxbridge is rising up. Stepped towers are at least more interesting than the old slabs in the centre, while the industrial estates march steadily outwards. Housing lines the towpath sides, so that one walks past an array of gardens, neat and trim, untidy or overgrown, old houses and new. There is a wharf with wharf cottages, and a working boatyard with a canopy carried on cast-iron pillars over the dry dock. Here one of the most famous of canal carrying companies – Fellows, Morton and Clayton – built and repaired their boats **(C)**.

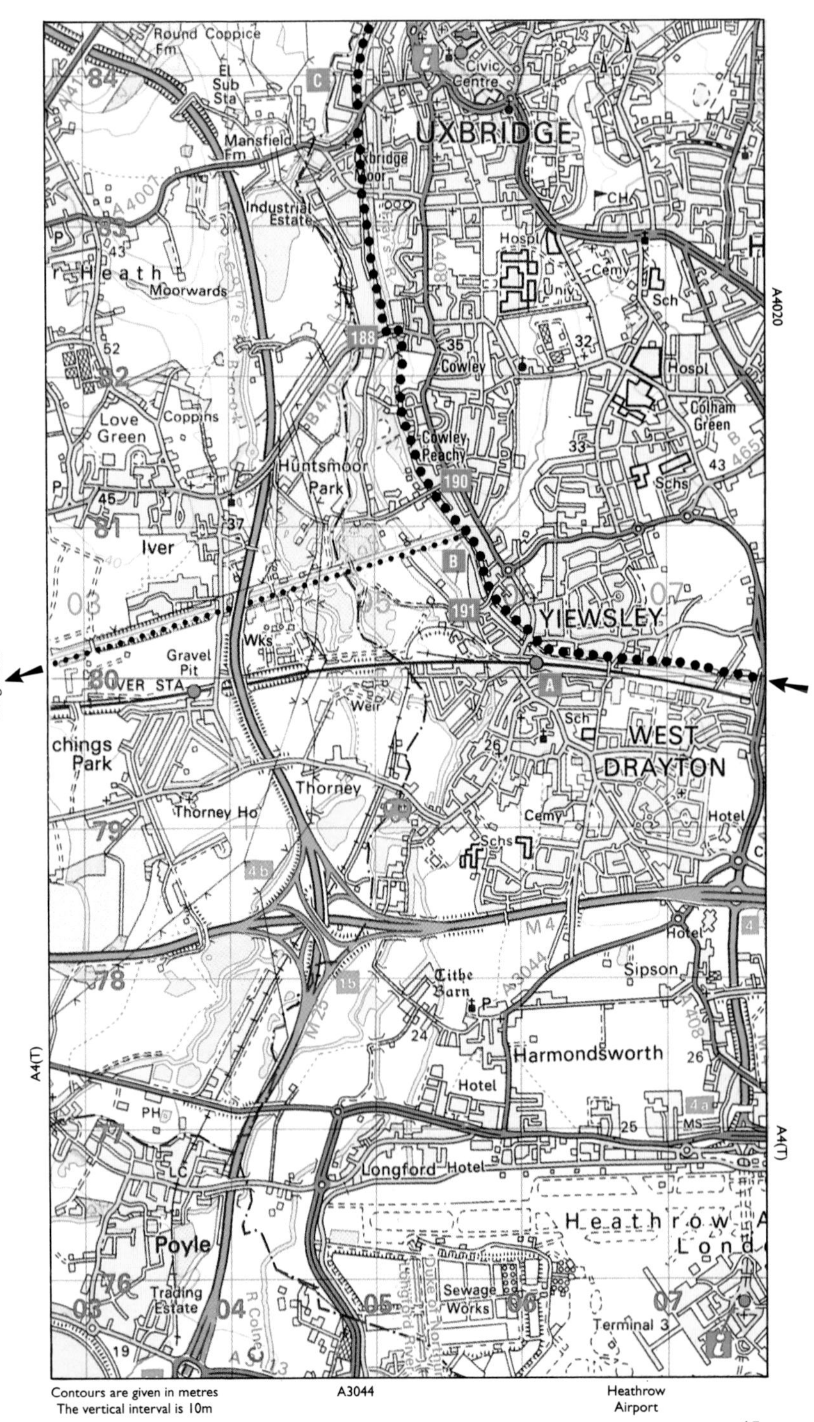

Round Coppice Fm
UXBRIDGE
Civic Centre
Mansfield Fm
Uxbridge Moor
Industrial Estate
Heath
Moorwards
Hospl
Univ
Cemy
Sch
A4020
Cowley
Love Green
Coppins
Cowley Peachy
Huntsmoor Park
Colham Green
Schs
Iver
YIEWSLEY
Slough Arm
Gravel Pit
Wks
IVER STA
Weir
WEST DRAYTON
chings Park
Thorney
Thorney Ho
Cemy
Hotel
M4
Tithe Barn
Sipson
M25
Harmondsworth
A4(T)
PH
Longford
Hotel
Heathrow
Poyle
Trading Estate
R Colne
Sewage Works
Terminal 3
Contours are given in metres
The vertical interval is 10m
A3044
Heathrow Airport

The old market town has been almost swamped by a rush to modernity, but it has at least been a wholehearted and determined rush. By far the most interesting of the new buildings stands right by the canal. *The Quays* has something of the look of a stranded Cunard liner, *circa* 1930, green and cream and curvy. There is a complex of waterways where canal and river meet. Immediately below the lock is Bridge 184, painted in a style that seems to challenge the modern exotica around it – whitewashed up to the string course, which is painted black; above that is plain brick with a blue brick parapet. On the left is the arm down which boats went to unload coal and load grain at the mill, then the river turns off and the waterway is again wholly canalized. Then comes the A40(M), a roar of traffic and a transformation scene. Instead of tight-packed buildings a series of small copses filled the spaces between the fields; we saw a horse standing in the shade of a horse chestnut. Up ahead the ground suddenly rears up around the aptly-named Denham Deep lock with its whitewashed cottage and black and white lock gates standing out sharply against the background of tall trees and grassy banks.

Beyond the lock a low aqueduct crosses Fray's River, while the Colne, overhung by willow, runs alongside. Now trees engulf the canal. Footpaths wind through the woodland, crossing the complex of streams on little wooden bridges **(D)**. It is quite easy to take a diversion here and rejoin the route a little further along. The woods are actually on the opposite side to the towpath, but that changes side at Bridge 182. In the woods, the raucous calls from a rookery compete with the noise of aircraft taking off from Heathrow. But the scene itself is tranquil, with glints from the water of lakes beyond the trees and sections of dense woodland; even the hard steel piling lining the canal has been softened by vegetation. A long straight leads up towards the railway bridge, a long viaduct, built on skew arches.

Now lakes, mostly formed from abandoned gravel pits, dominate the scene, and what must once have been eyesores are now transformed into attractive landscape features. Reed-fringed pools provide a home for a fleet of swans, while moorhen and coot scuttle around the edges. On the far side, a forest of masts announces the approach to the broad expanse of water of Harefield Marina. The arrival of the road bridge, Number 180, brings a touch of urbanity and Widewater lock. Office buildings and works appear to the right, but the string of lakes continues to keep the canal company on the left, as they will do all the way to Batchworth. Some are still worked for gravel, others have long been abandoned. Between lakes and canal is a ditch-like stream overhung by willow. The houses of Harefield finally end on the right, protected by an old pillbox, a reminder of days in the Second World War when the canal was not just a transport route, but a potential obstacle to an advancing invader.

The older workings now seem very natural as trees have grown at their edges and the small islands provide nesting places for a variety of fowl and convenient fishing posts for heron, with the broader expanses being used for water sports. Now the path curves away and the houses disappear from view. In summer, this is a busy spot with boats passing on the canal, water skiers and sailing boats out on the lakes: out of season it is all very tranquil, with a choice of view: a phalanx of tall poplar to the right; lakes and their colonies of birds to the left.

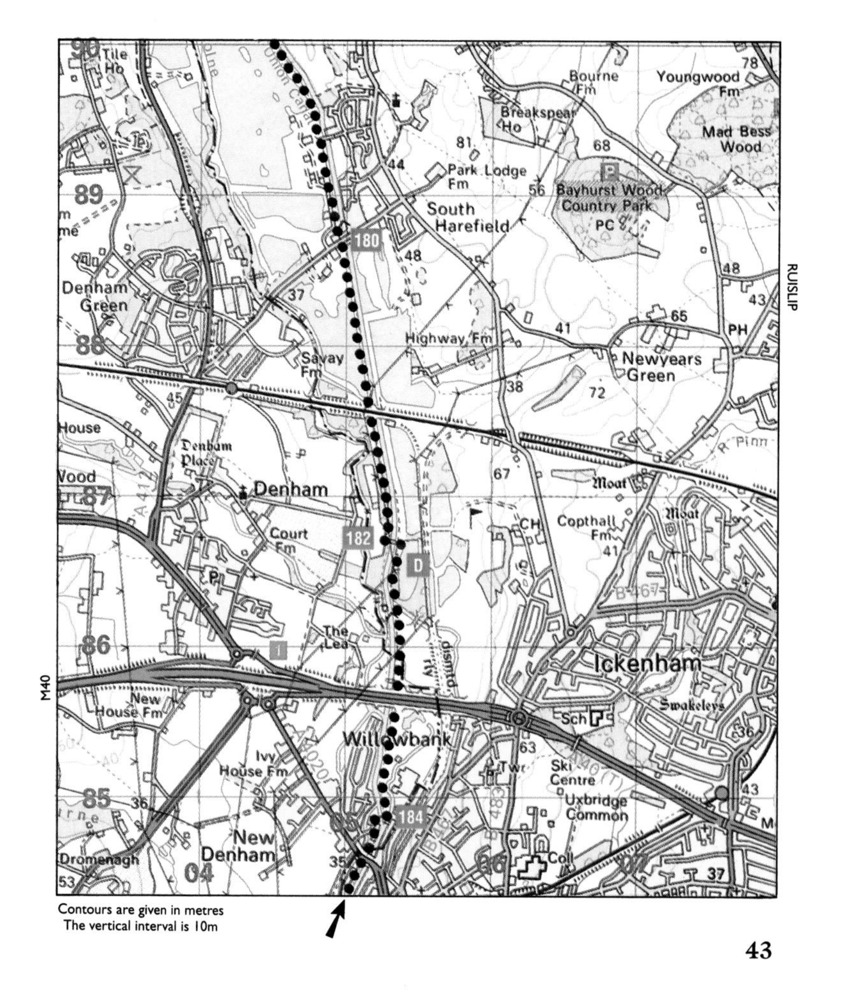

Contours are given in metres
The vertical interval is 10m

Winter scene at Stocker's lock.

Black Jack's lock announces its presence with the contrast between the brilliant white of the bridge arch and the black of lock gates beyond it. The setting is attractive, but night-time walkers beware – there is a resident ghost. Black Jack's Mill, which gives the lock its name, has been converted into a home, but the leat is still there and an attractive garden with a gazebo fills the space between canal and river. A brick bridge crosses the river, which turns out of the canal, tumbling over an odd, U-shaped weir. This is followed by a small working foundry and a new group of houses and flats. An iron bridge crosses an arm which once led to the old Troy Mill, then the path disappears into a green tunnel of drooping willow branches by Fishery Cottage. The canal goes through one of its extravagant kinks to emerge by the attractive *Fisheries Inn*, on an island site between canal and river. Next comes the large industrial complex of Copper Mill **(E)**, which, when the canal was new, manufactured copper sheeting for wooden boats to keep the dreaded marine worm at bay. The path beyond Copper Mill and Copper Mill lock shows large flint nodules, indicating that the outskirts of the wide band of chalk on the Chiltern Hills has now been reached.

Across the canal, the land now begins to rise in low, grassy hillocks, while nearer at hand the scene is dominated by the sewage works and a short arm which provides aromatic moorings. Beyond the works the Springwell reed beds are now a nature reserve, run by the Hertfordshire and Middlesex Wildlife Trust. Springwell lock has the now familiar pattern of a bridge, Number 176, across the tail of the lock and a small canal-oriented settlement, with an old industrial building, once used by Soya Foods, and a working pottery. Beyond is a pleasant wooded section and a now largely indecipherable stone pillar, which is actually an old Coal Duty stone, marking the point beyond which duty had to be paid on coal shipments heading to London.

The surrounding landscape is steadily becoming less flat and the canal must squeeze its way through the rising hillocks, at first heavily wooded then opening out to wider views. An attractive farm **(F)** surrounded by paddocks was once used for the filming of the TV series *Black Beauty*. It has great charm and shows a rich variety of building materials: weatherboarding, red tile softened by age and moss, rich, deep-hued brick. At Stocker's lock there is another two-level cottage, this time with a neat bay and a garden full of canal bits and pieces. The old gravel pits here have been transformed, with parkland round the edges and the water given over to sports as the Rickmansworth Aquadrome. This marks the beginning of another urban area, which starts with a new Tesco store – complete with moorings for boating customers. Rather like Uxbridge, Rickmansworth displays a complex of waterways, with the River Chess and its tributaries joining the canal. Frogmore Wharf was once home to Walkers, famous builders of narrow boats, and beyond it is the road bridge, Number 173, and Batchworth locks. This is an area full of interest. One lock continues the line of the canal, while a second leads into the River Chess. At the wharf is a charming group of buildings, one of which has been turned into a Canal Centre with an old Ovaltine boat, now a floating restaurant, moored outside. Above the locks a café and section engineer's house occupy an island site, and this is home base for an old narrow boat pair, named *Orpheus* and *Eurydice.*

A wooded section leads to a girder bridge and isolated Lot Mead lock, followed by a second railway bridge. It may come as something of a shock in such a rural setting to see the familiar silvery shape of a London tube train going across – but this is one of the further outposts of the Metropolitan line, serving Betjeman's

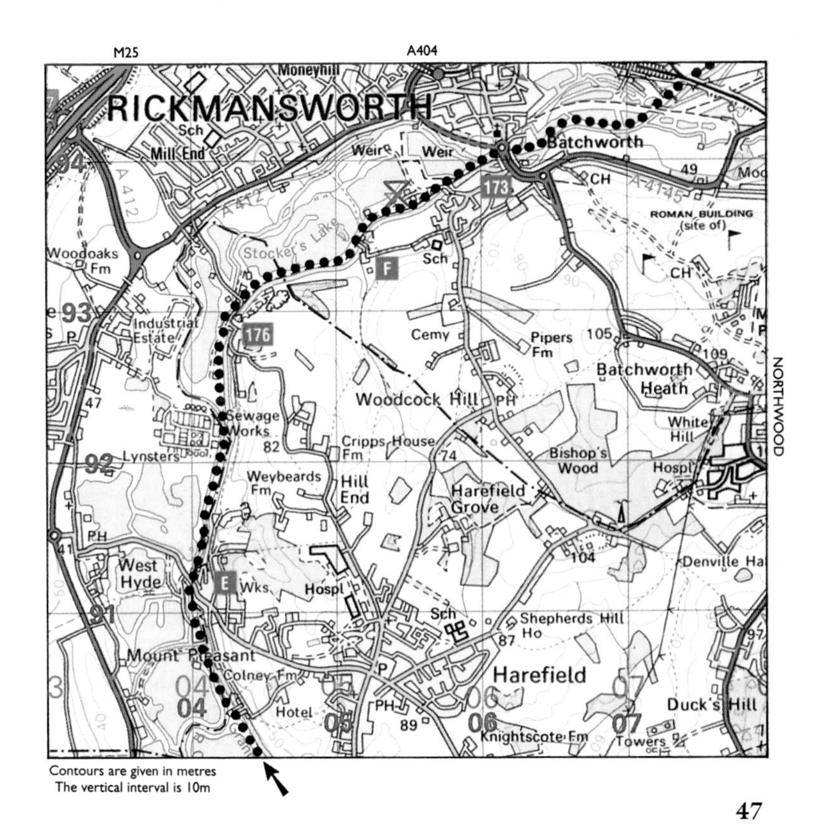

Contours are given in metres
The vertical interval is 10m

Former Ovaltine boat by the locks at Rickmansworth.

'Metroland'. The next section is what one thinks of as typical towpath walking, an enclosed strip bordered by hedgerows, with an occasional opening out to scrubby grassland along the valley of the Gade. Past Common Moor lock, building foundations indicate the site of the Croxley Paper Mills (**G**), once an important canal customer with a daily boat service to their depot at King's Cross. The canal is back in an urban area, but one almost hidden from view, with little more than gates to indicate that there are houses lurking behind the hedges. So rural does it still seem that it was no surprise to see a kingfisher fly out of one back garden, dip down to the water and fly on to visit a neighbour. Rows of neat wooden bridges over a ditch connect gardens to towpath. By a cluster of three bridges is a caravan park, whose principal occupants are gnomes; then a marina quite overshadowed by the immense railway viaduct. It is quite a contrast to the view ahead of Cassio Bridge lock and a delicate iron bridge, Number 168.

The lock marks a return to rural peace and quiet, and another reminder of the far-spread tentacles of the tube system with a row of London Transport houses. The canal swings gently now through woodland, largely dominated by waterside willow. On the towpath side, the trees rise up a low hill, while across the water the line of the reedy River Gade can just be discerned. Bridge 167 is different from the usual canal bridge in having a pointed arch, and as one approaches one can see how the steps leading up to the lock behind the bridge have been worn into graceful curves by generations of users. To one side now is Cassiobury Park, **(H)** while to the left a stand of tall beech trees marks the edge of Whippendell Wood. A little further on, a concrete 'distance post' announces that a lock lies just ahead. There are, in fact, two Cassiobury locks, and like the bridge before, the lock cottage is given extra ornamentation, this time in the form of castellation, to fit in with the parkland that was once part of the estate of the Earl of Essex. The towpath changes side past the locks and from the top of the turnover bridge there is a view of grand Grove House on the hill. At Bridge 165 the canal-side cottage is again ornamented, this time with round-headed windows. Then the canal twists and turns towards the most ornamental feature of all, the splendid balustraded Bridge 164, which was the price the canal company had to pay for passing through the aristocratic parkland of Grove Park, home of the Earls of

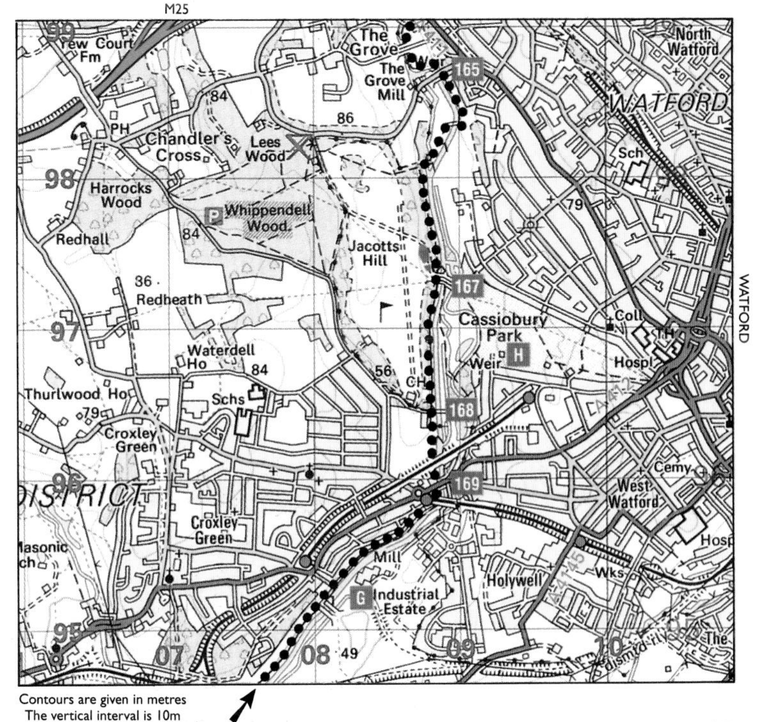

Clarendon, closely related to the neighbouring Essex family. Once clear of their lordships' land, the towpath changes back to its more usual side at Bridge 163.

The canal continues to twist round the edge of Grove Park towards Lady Capel's lock and a sad memorial to two men who died in constructing the Gade Valley sewer in 1970. The memories of an aristocratic past are even more firmly dispelled by the concrete bridge carrying a spur of the M25 joining the motorway to the A41. Two more locks carry the canal up past the village of Hunton Bridge, which remains tantalizingly just out of view, its centre indicated by the tall spire of the Parish Church. The area is, at least, served by two pubs at Bridge 162. Local materials predominate here – behind a wall of red brick, white brick and flint is a house of brick with tile-hung walls. This previously quiet rural area was dramatically changed with the arrival of the M25. Beyond Home Park Farm it sweeps over the canal on twin bridges, which are dramatic rather than graceful, before the scale of the landscape is reduced to more traditional proportions again on the approach to Kings Langley.

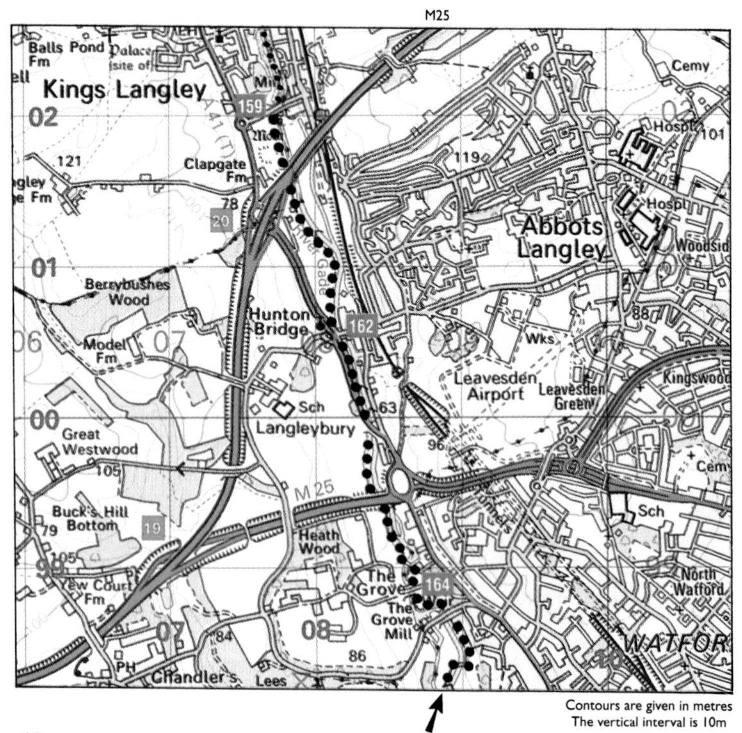

A Circular Walk to Whippendell Wood

3 $3/4$ miles (6 km) Allow 1 $1/2$–2 hours

Note: most of the woodland paths could be muddy after wet weather.

The walk starts from bridge number 167 by the Watford (or Ironbridge) Lock. Cassiobury Park Nature Reserve, run by the Hertfordshire and Middlesex Wildlife Trust, includes old water-cress beds, wetland, and woodland habitats which should be good for birds, plants and invertebrates. From the bridge there are several paths, but you take the track into the woods, turning right, or northwards, following close by the line of the towpath for a short distance. Then go left up the hill towards the sign which says 'Danger, Beware Golf Balls'. You continue straight on with a green and a hollow on your left, towards a gap in the trees ahead. You soon cross a private road which is not open to the public.

You are now on a lovely straight way through pleasant mixed woodland where you will find the occasional picnic table and rubbish bin. Where the main track veers to the right, just by the picnic tables, continue straight ahead, where there is a sign prohibiting horses, and continue going down hill. You are now in the lovely Whippendell Wood with a fine range of coniferous and deciduous trees, including hazel. You soon come to another clearing where tracks lead to right and left, but your way continues straight ahead. In the next little clearing the tracks appear to divide with one faint track forking off to the right but your way continues to the left. Follow the main, dirt path until, where you can see a group of slender silver birches, you turn off to the right on a grassy track and pass the birches on your left. Green woodpeckers yaffle and other birds, such as tits and finches, call.

The grassy track rises a little. Another woodland track joins you from the right but you carry on straight ahead and the going is muddy once more. Shortly afterwards, you should ignore a grassy track going off to the left and continue straight on along the muddier path, and you now begin to drop down a hill. The track forks once more and you keep to the muddier right side. You soon arrive at the road where the entrance into the woodland is barred by four posts.

Turn right on to the shady country lane. The road is overhung by trees, including horse chestnuts and beeches. Soon the woodland opens out a little and there are grazing meadows either side.

Ahead now you can make out the roar of the M25. By some rather ramshackle stabling, you emerge from Rouse Barn Lane on to the busier Fir Tree Hill Road, where you turn left. Ahead you can see the *Clarendon Arms* public house at Chandler's Cross. Almost opposite Chandler's Lane just before the Fir Tree Hill sign, and before you reach the pub, look out high up on your left for a public footpath fingerpost pointing to Croxley Green 1¼ miles distant. The entrance to the path, which is on your left, is rather overgrown and narrow. At first it runs between a barbed wire fence and a woven wooden fence on your right.

Soon the wooden fence is replaced by a beech hedge and then you enter Harrocks Wood through a wooden squeeze stile with a Woodland Trust sign on it welcoming visitors. Continue on along the broad woodland way which runs very straight ahead of you. There seems to be a chill in the air as you walk into this woodland of beech, birch, holly, ivy and ash. Pass between some rather odd cast-iron posts. Here and there, there are several more pairs of them. The path now descends a little and becomes gravelly underfoot. Just by a deep hollow on your right, you emerge

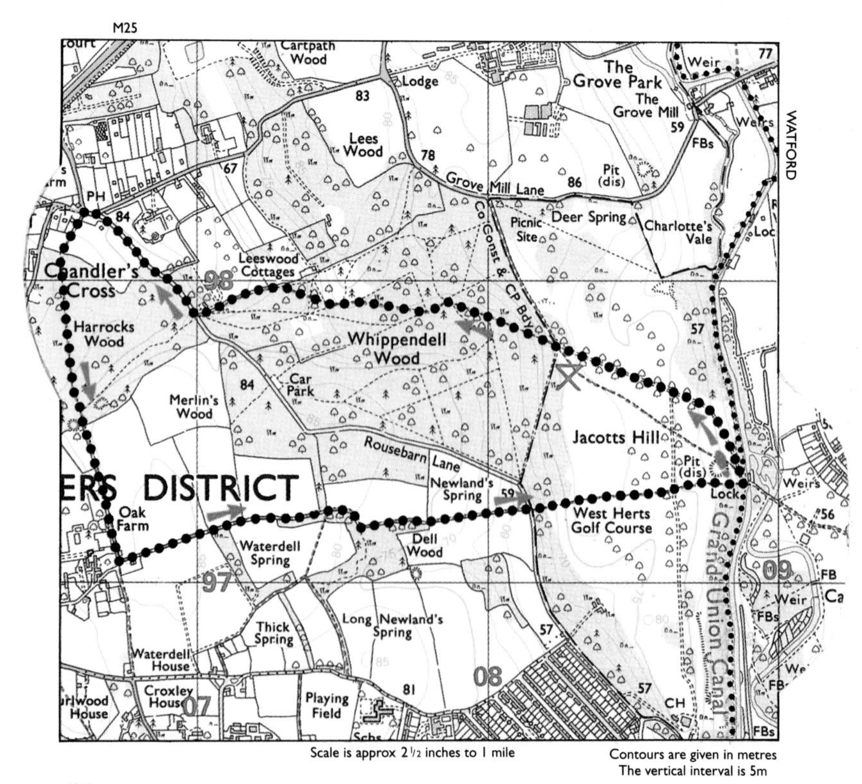

Scale is approx 2½ inches to 1 mile

Contours are given in metres
The vertical interval is 5m

from the wood again between a couple of wooden posts and on to a barbed-wire lined path with arable fields on your left and a meadow on your right. By a charming red-brick cottage, the path emerges on to a grass-centred, partly metalled lane where you continue straight ahead. You soon arrive at the collection of red-brick and prefabricated buildings that must be Redheath and, just after the Dutch barn that you will have seen earlier and before another barn, look out on your lefthand side for a stile and a public footpath sign.

Take this lefthand turn: the path can be rather overgrown in late summer, and hawthorns heavy with berries overhang the track. The hedges to left and right have gaps from time to time, revealing glimpses of Whippendell Wood ahead or of the fields to the right. Then the hedge on your left is replaced by a barbed-wire fence and there are older trees on your right. Dive back into the undergrowth once more, though it is a little more open than at first with the occasional, bulbous-trunked old oak. By a tall rowan tree, lovely with berries in the season, you come to a stile, and over it a broad farm track. There are paths off to left and right with Dell Wood on your right but your way continues more or less straight ahead towards the open field, keeping the woodland on your right. Follow the path as it bears round a little to the right and then left. Look out for grey squirrels scampering along the branches.

At the end of the wood, you come to a wooden stile and you simply follow the broad path across the arable field which was ploughed and harrowed as we passed through in late summer. Head straight for some dark-looking woodland and, on the horizon to your right by some tall poplar trees, there are the houses which mark the outskirts of Rickmansworth. The woodland ahead seems to clothe a longish ridge and almost to act as a barrier to your travels. Pass beneath a low wooden barrier, where there is a public footpath sign, on to a narrow road. Cross the road and go straight ahead into the woodland and up the hill. The going underfoot is stony and it is a moderately steep hill but you are soon at the top of the ridge and back at the golf course where once again your way is straight ahead and there is a sign warning of danger from golf balls.

Continue following the clearly defined path across the fairway towards the next patch of woodland. You are soon on the broad path through the trees. Cross a narrow partly metalled lane and continue straight ahead. You soon drop sharply down the hill towards the canal.

The Slough Arm

Beyond Bridge 191 cross the main line to join the branch. This was not one of the original branches off the Grand Junction of 1793, but was constructed almost a century later in 1882 – not quite the last canal to be built in Britain (that honour belongs to the Manchester Ship Canal) but next to it. Something of its modernity is obvious from the start, for it heads off for its objective with scarcely a wriggle along the way, as direct as the main London to Bristol line, Brunel's Great Western, that runs alongside for much of the way.

It begins with a very watery landscape of flooded gravel workings through which three natural waterways thread a route – Fray's River, the River Colne and Colne Brook, each of which is crossed by a low, iron aqueduct. Between, the first bridge carries a footpath off to the section of flooded workings known as Little Britain Lake **(A)**, now used for recreation and a haven for wildlife. Under the bridge is a small stone obelisk, a Coal Duty

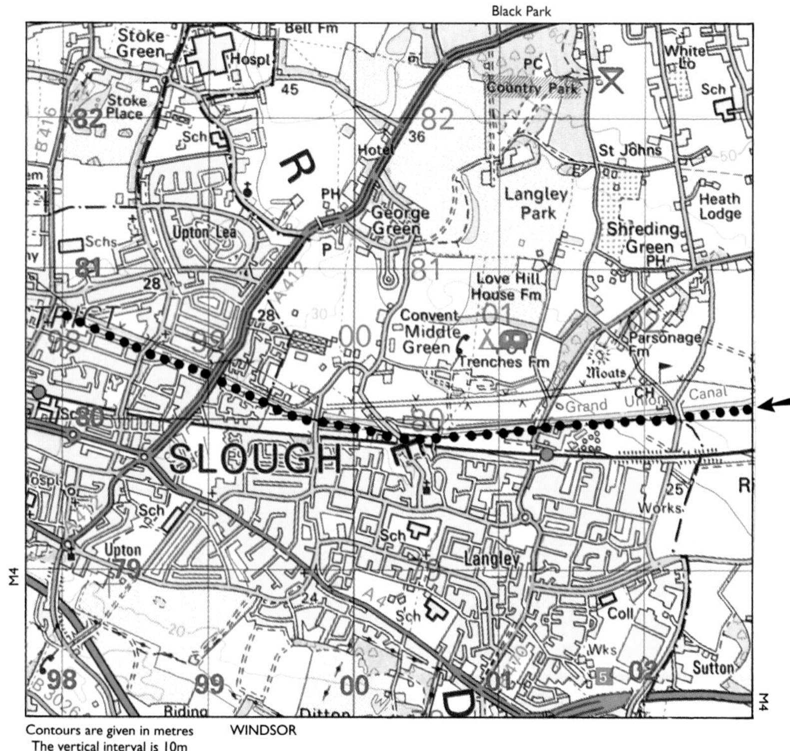

Contours are given in metres
The vertical interval is 10m

post indicating that any coal bound for the capital was liable for duty when it passed this point. It was redundant eight years after the canal was built, when the tax was abolished. The canal now passes under the massive, new bridge that carries the M25 before plunging into a long cutting that ends in a wilderness of disused gravel pits and waste land. But the passing of industry has left a rich habitat for wildlife. Moorhens graze on arrowhead, frogbit and pondweed; insects and fish shelter among the sweet flag and reed mace. Beyond the bridge that carries the footpath to Iver is a winding hole, then another bridge to be followed by the Iver golf course. Once the area was gravel pits, later filled in with London refuse brought here by boat, then restored.

More old pits follow at Langley, where there was a flourishing brick trade throughout the nineteenth century, and this was the area the canal was built to serve. After that the canal runs through the outskirts of Slough to a terminal basin by a timber yard. Rather than retrace your steps, it is possible to return by train from Slough station to West Drayton, close to Bridge 192 on the main line of the Grand Union.

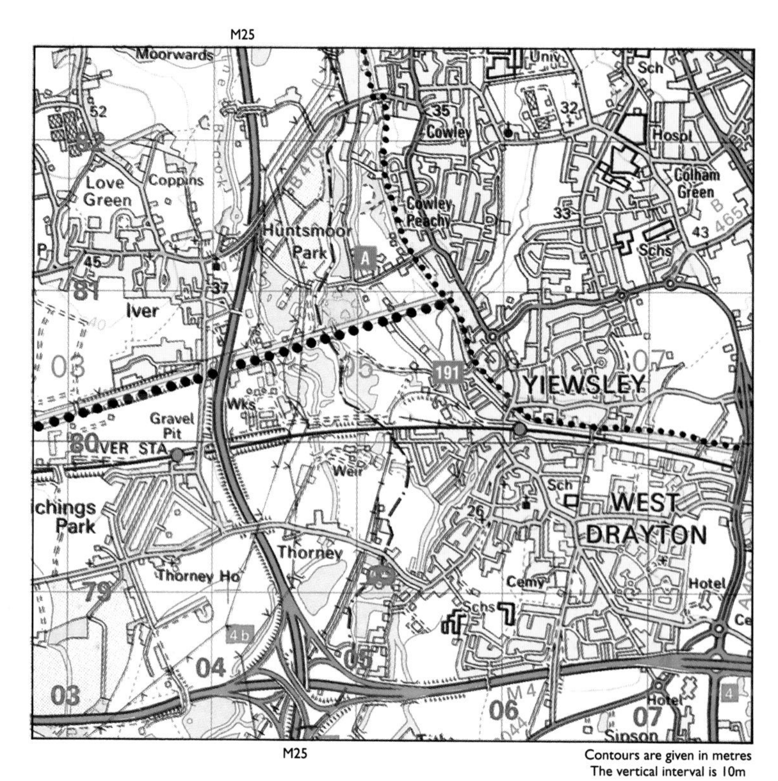

Contours are given in metres
The vertical interval is 10m

16 MILES (26 KM)

Pass beneath Bridge 159 and then under the concrete road bridge to arrive at a lock. On your left is the River Gade. On the far side of the river there is a lake and recreational area while, on the right bank, there are new houses and modern industrial buildings. Here and there small stands of *Phragmites* reeds line the canal side. Look out, too, for the trailing stems and green flowers of wild hops which adorn the hedgerows.

As you approach the complex of old and new factory buildings on the right bank, there is the sweet, delicious smell of chocolate in the air, aromatically announcing that Ovaltine **(A)** makes its famous bedtime drink here. The towpath passes between two little brick-built parapets crossing the river which here feeds the canal; to the left of the hedge the rumble and swish of passing trains is a reminder that the railway is just a stone's throw away.

You soon approach another concrete-spanned, brick-parapetted and iron-railed road bridge, Number 158. Cross it, and shortly before you reach the lock, the waters of the canal divide. The other channel is the former course of the canal, replaced, together with six original locks, in 1818 to placate the local paper mill owners. Pass by a weir and under a narrow iron footbridge which crosses from the towpath into an attractive modern housing development where there is also a secluded branch to the canal. The small back gardens of modern, box-like houses are blessed with an attractive watery boundary to their furthest edge but across to your left, the busy A41 is a reminder of the rushing workaday world. The canal is quite broad here and offers a ribbon of habitat for wildlife in this otherwise very built-up area.

The spick and span Ovaltine works at King's Langley.

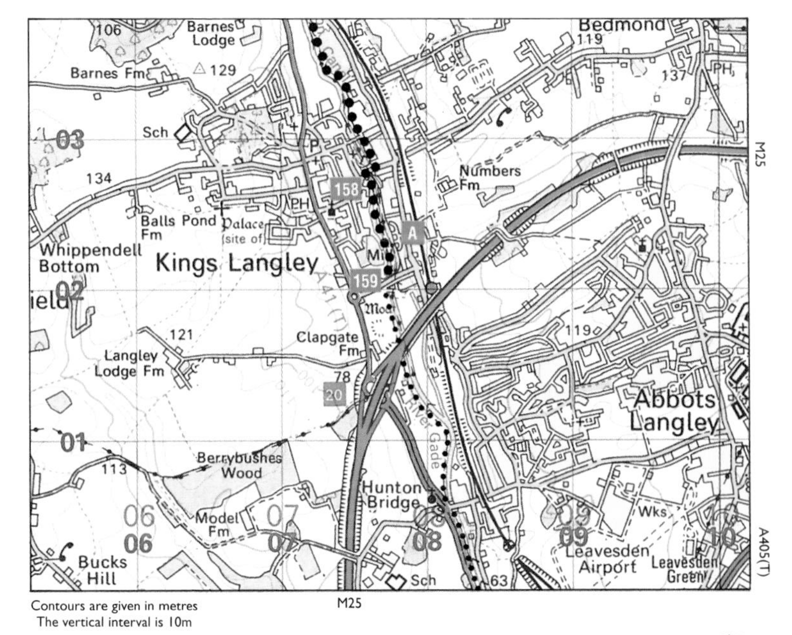

Contours are given in metres
The vertical interval is 10m

M25

Pass beneath an odd iron girder crossing the canal and then under the big skew bridge which carries the railway. Go under another steel affair, and the factories and tall buildings of Hemel Hempstead come into view. Just as you get to the next road bridge, the footpath seems to fork and the towpath takes you across a little wooden bridge keeping to the canal side. When you come to the road bridge, emerge on to the road and cross the bridge to pick up the towpath on the left bank. Pass by the old works buildings of Dickinson's paper mills **(B)** on your right and carry on towards Nash Mills Lock where the cream-painted brick lock-keeper's house still stands and offers the passer-by fine painted window boxes to cheer the way. Notice the quite spectacular glass office blocks with their landscaped, tree-fringed parking areas.

Ahead of you now, there is the newer and starker John Dickinson mill building, but graceful willows trail over the water to add a gentler touch. Pass beneath another iron contraption carrying pipes and, right beside the new mill buildings, an elegant, white-painted, double-arched bridge (154) comes into view: you make use of it to take you to the other bank of the canal. The forbidding, bare grey metal walls of the mill tower upwards, and enclosed corridors carry who-knows-what across the canal.

You now approach Apsley Locks where, once again, there are hedges of buddleia with their attendant butterflies – red admirals, meadow browns, tortoiseshells. To the left, there is a square church tower and spire, and before it as we passed by a chaos of rubble and big diggers portended the development of a new Sainsbury's supermarket. Look out for solitary moorhens or coots. Pass beneath a narrow concrete footbridge before reaching the next lock, as well as former canal company workshops. The white-painted brick span of Bridge 153, just before the lock, is supported by a half decahedron of ironwork. Cross the bridge to the left bank of the canal again.

On the right bank, houses have their back gardens reaching down to the canal, and vegetables and flowers grow in profusion. One, in particular, is ablaze with colour and busy with tables, gnomes, pedestals, seats, dovecotes and more. Carry on beneath Bridge 152 and look out on your right for the friendly *Albion* canal-side pub. The bridge looks a little the worse for wear while the rubbing bars seem barely worn. On the right bank now, park-like meadowland sweeps down to the water's edge. The towpath continues in good order and the townspeople of Hemel make use of it for relaxing strolls, while small boys cast their hopeful lines into the brownish-green water. Discarded cans bob alongside the young coots struggling to make headway with their lobed feet. Pass by a timber store on the right bank, announced a little earlier by the aroma of newly cut wood. This is next to a DIY centre.

Walk beneath the squared-off brick and concrete Bridge 151 and the canal takes you through a recreation ground where the River Gade branches off to the right. Pass by another lock with its old oak bollards, gnarled and pitted by countless ropes. On the right, fringed by waterside horse chestnuts, there is a cricket pitch, while to the left, there is more tree-dotted parkland – owned by Boxmoor Trust – with an old gas-holder beyond, a reminder of the days of coal gas. Go under another white brick and concrete bridge with an ironwork parapet, Number 150, which carries the A414. Walk by a low-rise, perhaps 1960s, development of flats and maisonettes on the right bank with its 'Private, No Landing' notices. Cross a little stream and look out for the orange flowers of Himalayan balsam among the willowherb.

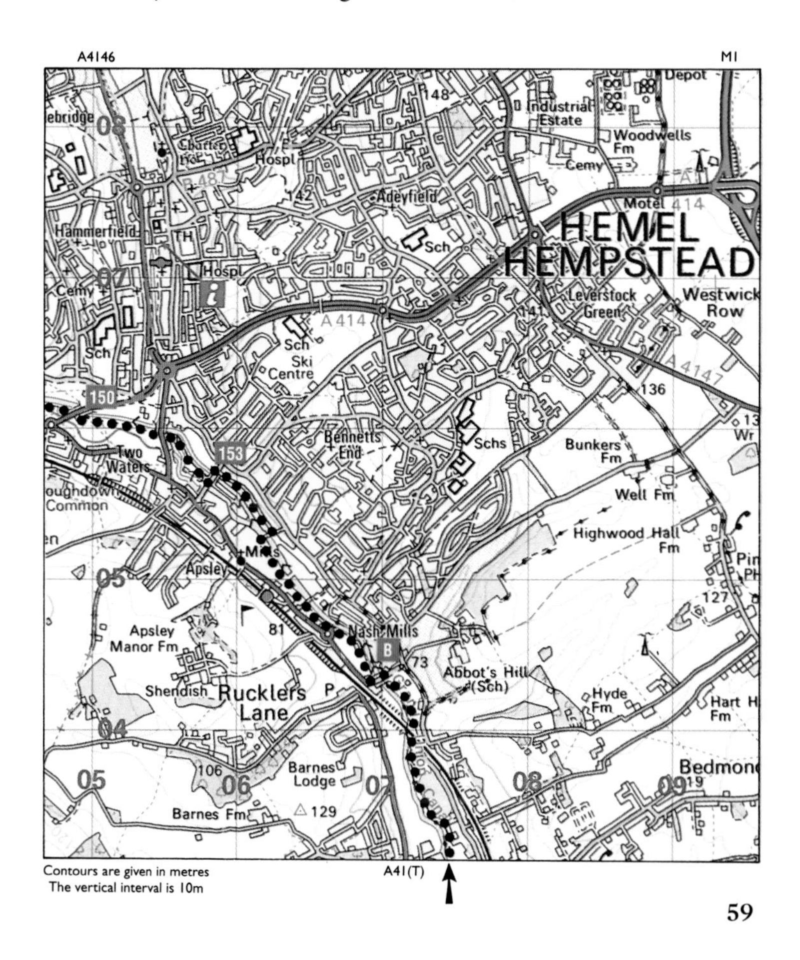

Next comes a stand of white willows with their pale, greeny grey leaves, and in the fields to the left horses graze peacefully. At the next concrete bridge (149) and lock there are the gardens and playing areas of the *Fishery Inn* on the right bank. Go under the bridge and past the lock where there are some old, rotting, and heavily pollarded willows. Pass beneath an iron, tracery-topped bridge supported on brick piers – this is Bridge 148. To your left there is a near-derelict house, and hard by on your left, on the other side of a marshy patch with its willowherbs, thistles, and buddleia, is the railway, its high embankment cloaked in lush vegetation.

You then approach Boxmoor Top Lock where a single-storey, white-painted, waterside cottage is protected at either end by conifer hedges and at its front by yew. Look out here for the disused watercress beds on the righthand side. For the moment, the canal is arrow straight, with more parkland and playing fields on the right. Before you pass beneath the railway, fine lawns backing comparatively modest houses slope down to the canal's right bank. Pass beneath the big, skew, brick and concrete railway bridge and beyond, serious, heavily equipped anglers are often found lining the bank during the fishing season. Pass by Lock 61, Winkwell Dock **(C)** which houses the Middlesex and Herts Boat Services. Winkwell swing bridge, key operated and numbered 147, could carry you across to the *Three Horseshoes* public house which claims to date from 1535. On the left now, as you approach Winkwell Lock, the gardens of canal terraces and brick-built bungalows crawl down to a little stream.

Note that, for the moment, you are heading westwards but, as you reach Bourne End, the canal bears round a little to the right. Cross the little wooden footbridge where the water to the left is overhung by willows, and you are soon at Lock 59. On the waterway to your left, notice the building that, until the 1930s, was a corn mill and has now been extended to find a new occupation as a hotel. Pass beneath Bridge 146 with its flaking white paint and well-worn rubbing bars. To the left there is a wilderness wasteland of what was once allotments; look out, hereabouts, for the drooping heads of comfrey as well as spear thistle and woody nightshade. Between the canal and the church at Bourne End there are some gravel workings and wetlands with reed mace and stands of goldenrod. You soon pass beneath Bridge 145. On the right is the railway and the square settlement beds of a sewage treatment works with the aptly named Sewerage Lock near by. Next you come to Lock 58 but, before you get

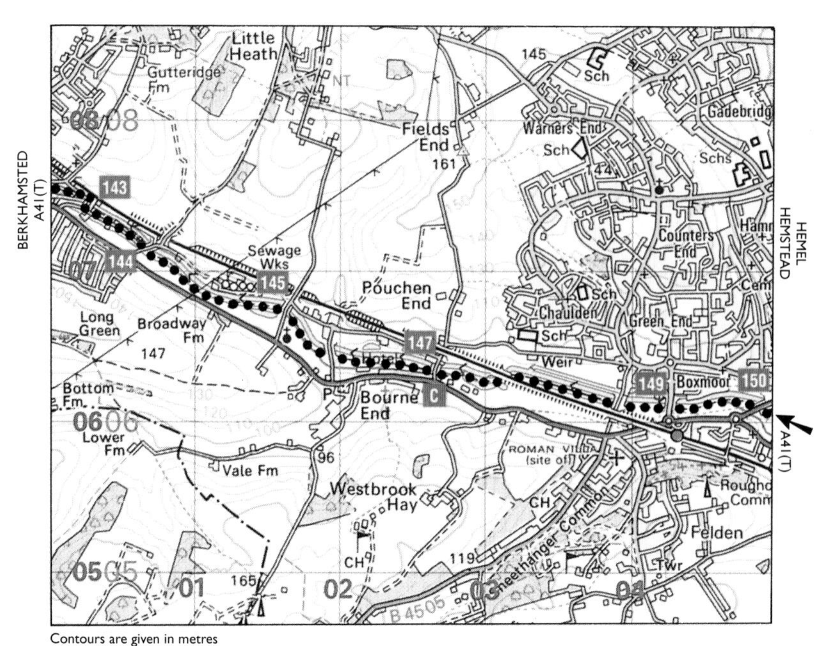

Contours are given in metres
The vertical interval is 10m

there, in late summer, there are some fine bushes of guelder rose with its red berries and three-lobed leaves. Earlier in the year, these would be adorned with umbels of white flowers. Here, too, there is the other red-berried shrub, wayfaring tree with its deeply veined oval leaves.

As you approach Lock 57 the busy A41 creeps ever closer and ever noisier while, beyond, arable fields climb the hill to the horizon. You soon arrive at Bridge 144. The towpath beneath the bridge has been reinforced with engineering bricks dated 1914. Then you pass by the pretty cottages of Bank Mill and Windlass. You are soon at Lock 56 with its tiny attendant cottage. Just beyond, in the paddock, as we journeyed, there was a small herd of fawn-coloured Toggenburg goats. There are splendid, almost copper-leaved trees overhanging the canal among the more common sycamore, willow and sweet chestnuts which virtually conceal the tennis courts behind.

Pass beneath Bridge 143 and the path takes you around and over it to join the right bank just in front of a 1930s-style bungalow. Then you can see that a small canal-side warehouse with its flagstone landing stage has been converted, in part, to private apartments. Here the towpath is hemmed in with garden escapes such as goldenrod and Michaelmas daisy, as well as mallow. Go under a single span of concrete carrying a footbridge before approaching the more industrial outskirts of Berkhamsted. The stump of an old chimney beside a square-towered church can be seen rising above the buildings. The next lock is 55 with Bridge 142 beyond. Here is the excellent canal-side *Rising Sun* **(D)** which was once a grocer's and alehouse before being granted a full spirit licence. Then you come to the larger and grander *Boat Inn* hard by the bridge and lock. Just beyond is Bridgewater Boats, then comes a timber yard with its extraordinary canal-side totem pole. Across the canal is the *Crystal Palace* pub, followed by Bridge 141.

Cross the canal using the bridge and you are on the left bank once more. Opposite, the railway is carried along a narrow-arched viaduct to Berkhamsted station. Berkhamsted Castle, hidden behind the railway, was an important Norman fortress, and it is now in the care of English Heritage. William the Conqueror received the offer of the English Crown here in 1066. The castle stood within two moats but only a few flint walls remain.

Then the canal is crossed by a painted iron bridge with its accompanying piping just before the start of Berkhamsted locks. Go beneath a gently curving wooden footbridge. Along here there may often be more pedestrians than boats for the towpath is popular with local residents. On your left you have the River Bulbourne. Pass beneath another gently curving footbridge, this time constructed from dreary concrete and battleship-grey railings, which marks the end of the playing fields. You then arrive at a set of two locks (51 and 52) where there are low-rise flats and maisonettes beside the canal.

Next comes the ugly little Bridge 140 with its single concrete span on brick piers. On either side of Lock 39, where water flows over the sluice, the houses and industrial buildings are hidden by a screen of trees. Here the towpath is tarmacked, which keeps the boots clean but is a little hard on the feet. Immediately on your left are the backs of modern houses and, on the right, a rough meadow fringed with willowherb and goldenrod.

Pass beneath the old Bridge 139 with its relatively recent repair, and immediately beyond is Northchurch Locks. The countryside now begins to open out and pleasant rolling agricultural land is bounded by woodland fringes on the distant hill tops. Pass by a development of retirement homes and look out for the purple flowers of water mint as well as white dead nettle. Almost imperceptibly, the going underfoot has faded from hard tarmac to gravel as you approach Bridge 138. Cross it to take to the right bank by the lock.

The path is now a grassy way. Walk by Dudswell Lock (47) where, as we strode, another shimmering kingfisher sped past straight and true. Pass by the attractive black-and-white iron Bridge 137 at Cowroast where there is a lock beyond. On your left there is the *Cow Roast Inn* and there is a variety of facilities for canal goers. Cross the little bridge, where the inlet leads to a big marina, to continue on your way. Here there are Tring Summit Visitor Moorings.

Two tall conifers stand guard over Bridge 136. The building on the lefthand side, after the bridge, is a Government 'Buffer Depot' holding emergency food supplies in case of national crisis. Now the towpath narrows because of the width of the hedgerow and becomes more broken and overgrown. On the other side, the banks are high and the undergrowth thick, draped in old man's beard. As you near Aldbury and Bridge 135 at Tring Station, it is as though you are walking along a dark-green leafy corridor. The bridge carries the route of the Ridgeway National

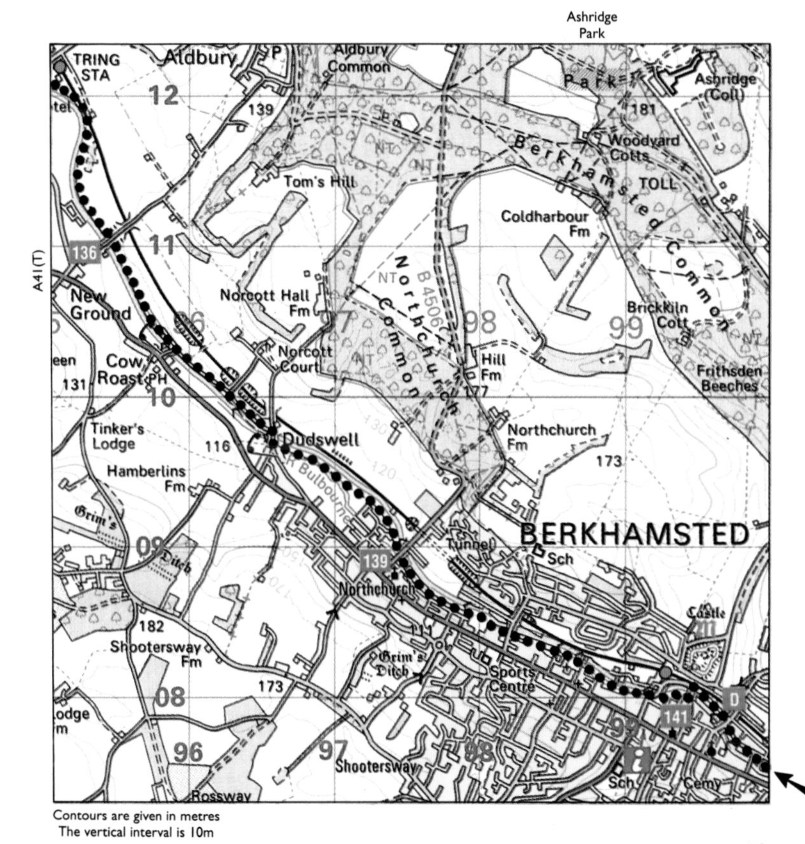

Contours are given in metres
The vertical interval is 10m

Trail **(E)** high above the canal. This stretch of water is known as Tring Summit Level. Tring is also the home of the British Trust for Ornithology and the British Museum (Natural History) reserve collection.

At the high, ivy-clad Bridge 134 the towpath moves to the other bank and there are the red berries of cuckoo pint standing out brightly among the dark green, bankside stinging nettles. Near the Upper Icknield Way Bridge (133) a speckled wood butterfly flitted along the undergrowth. Go under the brick-built bridge and, on the opposite bank, you will see the British Waterways Bulbourne workshops. Look out here for new wooden lock gates being made and soaked in the canal. Pass by a barbecue area, and you soon arrive at Bulbourne Junction where the Wendover Arm forks to the left and, on the main route, there is a flight of seven locks – the Marsworth flight. Marsworth and its lock have been known to generations of boaters as 'Maffers'.

Cross the bridge which takes you over the Wendover Arm and follow the signpost at the dry dock towards Braunston, 55 miles distant. As you reach the central locks, to your left there are reservoirs laid out for recreational purposes, with fine stands of *Phragmites* reeds. Boats tend to be concentrated here because of the number of locks, but it is also popular with strollers, anglers, picnickers, or those who just wish to sit and stare. These are the Tring Reservoirs **(F)**. To avoid drifting off your route and on to the Aylesbury Arm, it is best to cross the canal on the footbridge at the bottom lock, adjoining the Lower Icknield Way as it passes over the distinctive double-arched Bridge 132. Originally, the bridge had only one arch but traffic on the canal was so heavy that, in 1838, duplicate single locks were built from Bulbourne Junction through to Stoke Hammond. Several bridges then had to be extended with a second arch. Further north, the Stoke Bruerne flight of locks had been duplicated in 1834, again resulting in a double-arched bridge.

There is the *White Lion* pub right by the bridge and there are towpaths on either side of the canal. You now need to cross Bridge 131 on to the left bank, and here there is a British Waterways office. Go beneath Bridge 130 with its sign advertising the *Red Lion* and you pass by a licensed grocery shop in a charming thatched and timbered building.

Pass beneath the old brick Bridge 129 where the rubbing bar is deeply worn. Locks 37 and 38 are ahead. To the right the tall chimneys of Pitstone Cement Works mar the scene. You soon come to Dunstable and District Boat Club Moorings and the canal makes a sharp turn to the right, heading towards Bridge 126 and the railway lines. To the right, over the bridge, there is the *Duke of Wellington* pub and Pitstone Wharf Canal Centre with its coffee and souvenir shop. Pass by the swing bridge, Number 125, and Ivinghoe Beacon is on your right. You soon arrive at the first of the three Seabrook locks, and clover and yarrow grace the grassy path. From Ivinghoe Bridge, Number 123, the B488 gives access to Cheddington and Cheddington Station to the left, and Ivinghoe to the right. At Ivinghoe, there is the Ford End Watermill to visit while Pitstone, near by, has its windmill, and Ivinghoe's neighbour, Pitstone Green, boasts a farm museum.

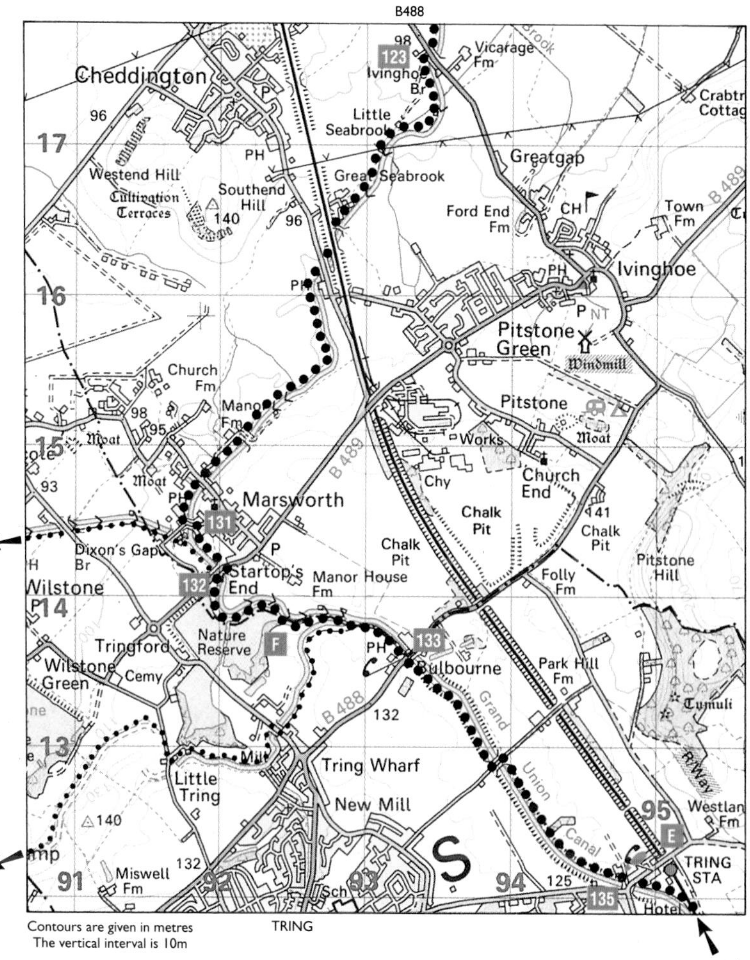

THE WENDOVER ARM

6 miles (10 km)

Note: in places the going underfoot can be very wet and/or muddy after rain.

The Wendover Arm begins its journey at Bulbourne Junction where it is signposted 'Wendover, 6½'. The arm was opened in 1797 after construction began in 1793, authority to make it navigable having been given in a 1794 Act of Parliament. It was intended mainly as a feeder to supply the summit level of the Grand Junction Canal with water from the Chiltern Hills. Water supplies were hardly adequate, however, so that they were augmented by building Wilstone, Marsworth, Tringford and Startopsend Reservoirs (see map p. 70) while the Weston Turville Reservoir was built by the canal company to compensate local millers for the loss of headwater which was diverted from Well Head to the Canal. Because the arm is built on porous chalk, water leaked from the channel and a stop lock had to be built at Tringford. By 1904, the section from Tringford to Drayton Beauchamp was drained. In the 1960s, much clearance work was carried out by British Waterways and the Manpower Services Commission to open up the canal to the public. In spring and autumn especially, this arm makes for a particularly lovely stroll through typical English countryside. And the dewatered section between Little Tring and Drayton Beauchamp is like a sunken haven for nature, almost a ha-ha gone bush!

Pass beneath the single-span iron bridge and make your way along the towpath. Already, this is a very river-like stretch of canal with brambles, willow, hawthorn, monk's rhubarb, willowherb, nettles and more adorning the way. You can soon see Startopsend, Marsworth and the Tringford Reservoirs on your right. Beyond, in the far distance, is the conurbation of Aylesbury, while all around is pleasant, open, tree-fringed countryside. A slight scent in the air portends, as do the flocks of wheeling gulls, the distribution beds of a nearby sewage farm. Pass by the works on your right towards the village of New Mills on the outskirts of Tring. Here you can still see the old, brick-built flour mill but by the canal bridge there are buildings that were once part of Bushell Brothers, the boat builders who also owned the wharf.

You must leave the towpath for the moment to go over a stile and on to the road. Cross the canal on the bridge and then continue on the towpath, on the right bank this time, passing by corrugated steel warehousing on your left. As we walked by, a steel wide boat was tied alongside the wharf. Just beyond the mills there are some little brick bungalows and you are on the edge of a small housing estate. Then comes a collection of ramshackle, corrugated iron huts. Soon, though, to right and left, there are lovely open fields once again but the grassy towpath is somewhat uneven.

By a white cottage, now sporting an incongruous black satellite dish, you pass through an iron gate and you come to Tringford pumping station **(A)** with its square, brick, keep-like house that once contained a Boulton and Watt steam engine. You have now reached the end of the navigable section of the canal and you can still see the old stop lock here, although it is silted up. Walk around the head of the navigation and carry straight on towards the road. Just before some steps leading up to the road, bear right up the track and join the road there. Turn right and walk by the pleasant red-brick cottages of Little Tring.

Less than 100 yards along the road, look out on your lefthand side for a public bridleway sign pointing left up a farm lane. You then come to a pair of gates; follow the footpath beside the dewatered navigation which is now rich in undergrowth. Your

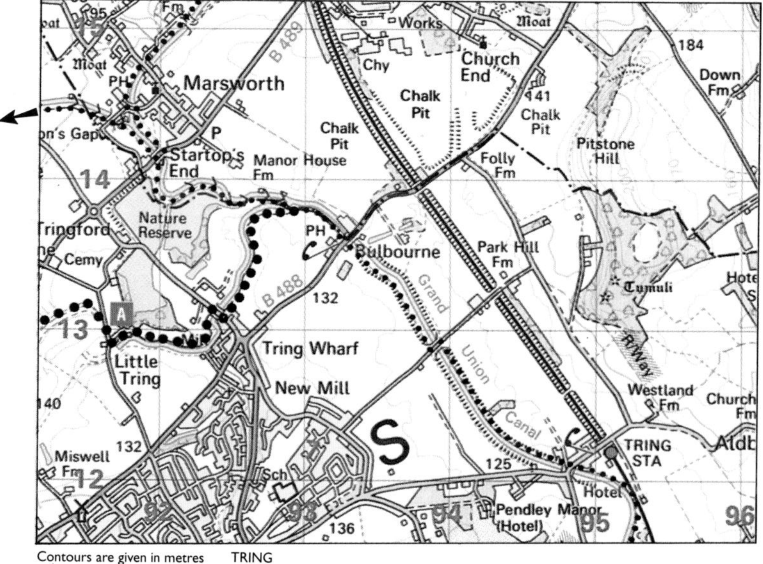

Contours are given in metres
The vertical interval is 10m TRING

way follows the channel, bearing left while ahead to the right there is Wilstone Reservoir Nature Reserve, the waters sparkling azure in the late autumn sunshine as we walked by.

At a crossing of the ways, where there is a smart wooden finger-post, continue straight on. Ahead cars' glinting paintwork climbing rapidly uphill announces the nearby road rising through Drayton Beauchamp while woods brood darkly on the horizon ahead. Almost imperceptibly at first, the noise from the busy A41 ahead loudens, but first there is the small collection of buildings on the outskirts of Drayton Beauchamp, and you come to a minor road. Before you get to the road, however, (unless you stop to look at the fifteenth-century Drayton Beauchamp church **(B)**), there is a track leading down towards the canal channel so that you can walk under the bridge.

You are now walking through a leafy cutting where the canal is still dewatered. In autumn the colours are splendid. Gradually, however, the channel begins to grow damper and then starts to fill with water. Then you reach the sluice where the canal water disappears down a sump to feed into Wilstone Reservoir. The path is now flat and even and dry, and soon become partially metalled as you approach the hamlet of Bucklandwharf between Aylesbury and Tring. The channel is well silted up, and the water is very shallow but crystal clear. Just before you get to the A41, by a narrow accommodation bridge, leave the canal side using a stile, cross the narrow road, and continue on the canal-side track. On your left is the large, square *Homesitters* pub.

Cross the busy road, using caution, and look out for the canal-side path.Cross over another little stile to continue on your way. On your right, there are tiny modern bungalows many of which have pretty water gardens. Pass beneath the brick-built arch carrying the B489 road and, once again, you are walking through a lovely, leafy, watery avenue.

Pass beneath an old accommodation bridge where steps will take you up on to the road if needs be. Above the filtration beds of a sewage farm to your left, the tail fin of an aircraft rises incongruously to announce the presence of an airfield, and you soon come to the beautifully kept, open playing fields that are MOD property. Pass beneath a splendid tracery ironwork, blue-painted bridge bearing the Rothschild emblem in gold. Then comes the rather more mundane concrete and iron bridge carrying the minor road through Halton village. Here you must cross a stile on to the road, cross the bridge, and continue along the footpath on the right bank beside a Dutch-roofed, white-painted cottage.

With the centre of Aylesbury away to your right, you now pass by a large, open, grassy field and on your left there is a housing estate on the far side of the tall trees. The canal makes a sharp turn to the left. Pass beneath another tracery iron bridge on brick piers; this again carries the minor road into Halton. With the houses of Wendover in sight ahead, the canal suddenly widens and then becomes silted up again, providing a home for fine stands of reed-mace. As you approach Wendover, the canal-side path becomes a favourite with dog-walkers, and you are soon among the playing fields and meadows on the edge of the town. In 1993 Buckinghamshire County Council began a scheme to provide better car parking, disabled access, and interpretation, as well as a more substantial walking surface. Your way finishes by a little sluice where the waters disappear into a concrete tunnel beneath the road.

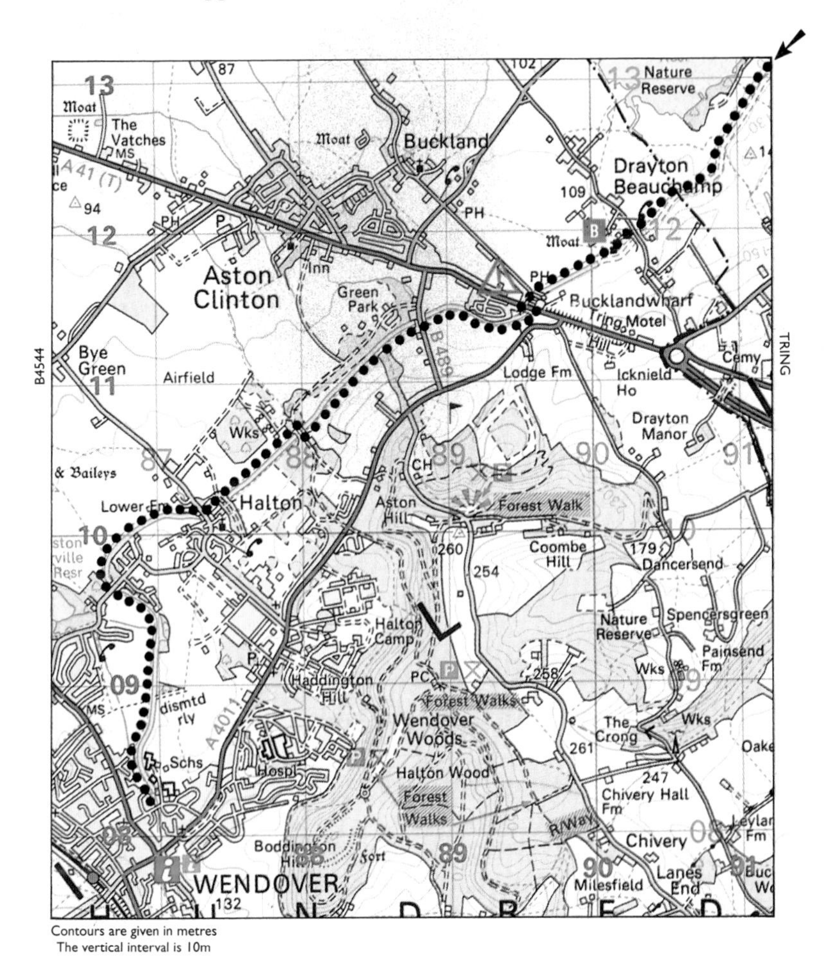

Contours are given in metres
The vertical interval is 10m

The Aylesbury Arm

The arm was originally destined for greater things, part of the 'Western Junction Canal' that would extend to the Thames at Abingdon where it would link with the Wilts and Berks Canal. It was opened as far as Aylesbury in 1814, and there it stopped.

The arm leaves the main line between Bridges 132 and 131 at Marsworth Junction. Turn left towards the two locks, joined together to form a staircase: unlike the locks on the main line, these are narrow, designed to take just a single boat. Seven more conventional locks now follow in quick succession. Bridge 3, immediately above Lock 8, is a road bridge leading into the nearby village of Wilstone. At Bridge 5 a small feeder stream provides water for the locks from Wilstone Reservoir **(A)**. The locks take the canal down to the broad expanses of Aylesbury Vale, dotted with black poplar, which are unusual in having been pollarded up to a height of 15–20 feet (4.5–6 metres). The canal itself runs almost arrow straight, but is seldom dull. In summer the waterside is busy with birds and abundant dragonflies and damselflies, while in winter the often wet, low-

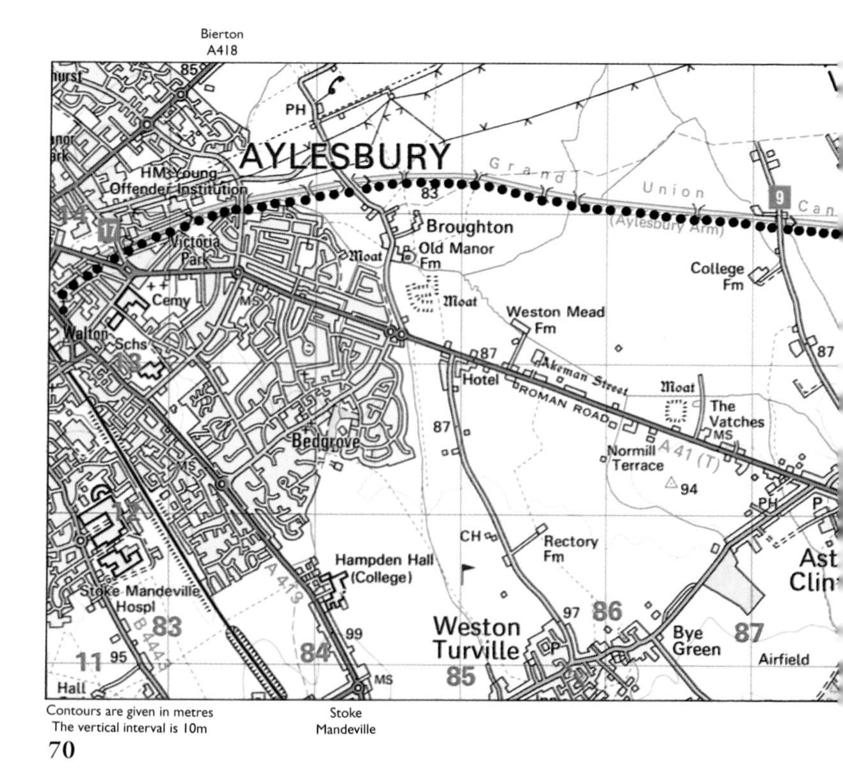

lying land is popular with many species, including migrant red-wing and fieldfare.

Two more locks continue the descent at Puttenham, and the walk continues to give wide views over a rural landscape of neat fields and hedgerows. Another pair of locks appears between Bridges 8 and 9, the second, Redhouse Lock, taking its name from *The Redhouse* pub, now a private house. The canal is now lock-free for two miles, the only interruption being a succession of small bridges. Broughton Lock marks the start of the last descent towards Aylesbury, with, first, attractive parkland and then a screen of willow and alder concealing the light industries that spread out from the town centre. The end of the arm is extensively used for moorings with boats lining both sides of the waterway. At Bridge 17 the Nestlé works appear, originally built by the Aylesbury Condensed Milk Company in 1870 to take advantage of canal transport. Aylesbury itself is an ancient market town, but little of its old character is shown here. The basin at the end occupies an exposed position at the edge of the ring road, surrounded by rather undistinguished office buildings. The old *Ship Inn* and one small warehouse survive as reminders of the days of the working boats.

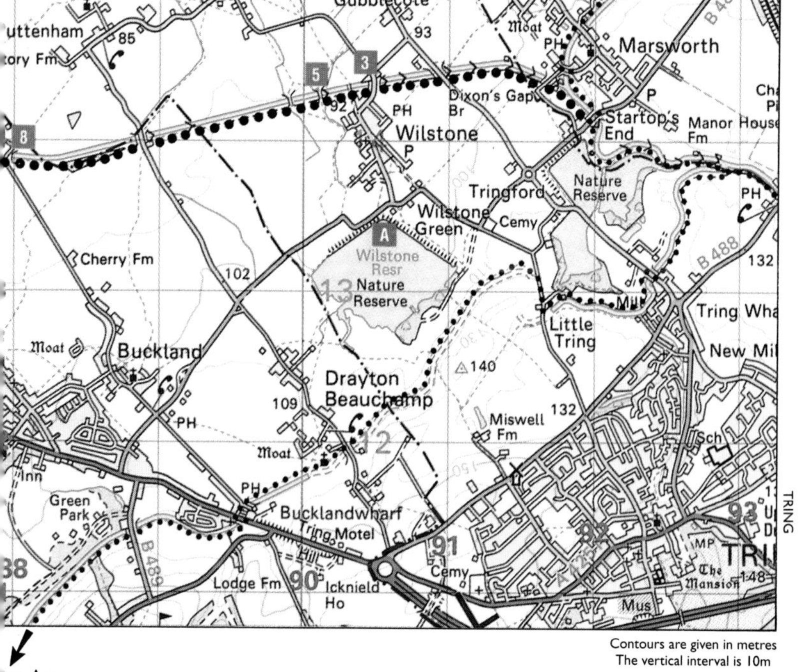

Contours are given in metres
The vertical interval is 10m

Graham Greene

Berkhamsted seems an unlikely birthplace for a writer whose work is generally set far from the Home Counties. When one thinks of Graham Greene, one thinks of Harry Lime lurking in the Viennese shadows, of drunken priests in South American villages or a train rattling through Europe in which every compartment seems to contain a spy. Yet Greene began the first volume of his autobiography, *A Sort of Life*, with these words: 'If I had known it, the whole future must have lain all the time along those Berkhamsted streets'. And in the first paragraph he speaks of the Grand Junction Canal – still the Grand Junction when Greene was born in 1904. His father was headmaster of the local school, and the author's earliest memories were of being taken out on walks by 'the crochety nurse' or a nursemaid. One of the regular trips was along the canal towpath, a walk of which Greene has no fond memories. He saw some romance in what he described as 'the painted barges' and the 'gypsy children', but mostly he felt menaced by dark-faced boatmen who spat out their resentment of the middle-class parade. He also had a special dread of the locks, with their sheer, dripping walls which gave him nightmares of drowning. But perhaps something else of canal life crept into his soul – the love of travel, a restlessness, a fascination with the lives of people so unimaginably different from that of his own respectable family.

Graham Greene was educated at Berkhamsted School and the role of headmaster's son was not one that he enjoyed. He once started to write a book with a school setting, but abandoned it to go to a leper colony in Africa, an experience that he found less harrowing than attempting to recreate his schooldays. His first published novel, *The Man Within*, now hardly ever read, did well, but he had to wait many years before he could match its modest success. It is hard to imagine the author of *The Power and the Glory*, *The End of the Affair*, some of the most powerful novels of the century – or indeed the author of the delectable 'entertainments', *Our Man in Havana*, or *Travels With My Aunt* – having spent ten years in the literary wilderness, but he did. Yet Graham Greene's life was always one of paradoxes and contradictions. The child who was terrified of the sight of a canal lock become the young man who would go out with a loaded pistol for solitary games of Russian roulette. The most famous writer on Catholicism in Britain had his books banned by the Catholic Church. And the exile who lived abroad and restlessly travelled the globe could write in his sixties of his love for the landscape around Berkhamsted.

Tring Reservoirs and Wildlife on the Grand Union

Like their later – and ultimately successful – rivals, the railways, canals were constructed as commercial, working highways, with little or no thought of their value to the natural world. And like railways, once again, they have matured over the decades, so that throughout their routes, and especially where they pass through urban areas, they resemble very long and rather narrow nature reserves. Unlike railways, however, canals, by their very nature, add one further dimension to their role as wildlife havens – water. While so many of our rivers are suffering through pollution, eutrophication, silting, overuse as sources of drinking water, or choking through the invasion of alien plants, the proper management of canals and their towpaths has enabled them to survive and prosper both as habitat for all kinds of wildlife and as leisure facilities for boat-users, anglers, casual strollers or dog-walkers, and, in the case of the Grand Union Canal, for the long-distance walker.

Even the most casual observer on the Grand Union cannot fail to notice some of the more conspicuous signs of its abundant wildlife. In spring and autumn, the trees and hedgerows are at their most attractive with willows, gnarled and aging or vigorous and graceful, lining many stretches of the banks. And there are plenty of other species of tree too from stately horse chestnuts and oaks to elders and alders, wayfarer's tree and guelder rose, the latter covered in white blossoms early in the year which are replaced by clusters of red berries in late summer. Various species of bramble are, of course, commonplace and these may be draped by bryony, old man's beard or even hops. Stands of *Phragmites* reed or reedmace grace the banks and silted-up winding holes from time to time while, in the water, there are pondweeds, soft rush and arrowhead. And by the towpath, clover, cow parsley and other umbellifers, vetches, scabious, willowherbs, spear thistles, buttercups, bedstraws, medick, cuckoo-pint, goldenrod and many other plants add colour and luxuriance to the scene.

Many of Britain's commoner butterflies can be seen along the canal, especially where there are shrubs like buddleia to provide them with nectar and pollen. Gatekeepers, meadow browns, tortoiseshells, cabbage whites and peacocks are probably the most likely species to be seen but you may even come across rarities like the Essex skipper butterfly, at the north-western limit of

Sunset over Tring reservoir.

its range near New Bradwell. On the ground, a disturbed devil's coach-horse may raise its tail in defiance while damselflies and dragonflies clatter through vegetation only to buzz away in a shimmer of blue, black or rusty brown.

Fish have been mentioned in the feature on angling, but there is plenty for the ornithologist on the canal. Mallard, coots, and moorhens are as common here as on any other watery site, and it

is hard to walk more than a few hundred metres without putting a grey heron heavily to flight. In some places, swans may have built their substantial nest right by the towpath, and sitting adults may well intimidate the more cautious passer-by. In summer, swallows and martins hawk for flies over the canal or dip their bills in the water to take a drink as they fly. But perhaps the highlight of the canal is the number of kingfishers to be seen along its length. Seeming almost out of place by the brownish-green waters of an English waterway, the brilliantly coloured kingfisher is surprisingly numerous. More often than not, you will see it as a blaze of azure and copper, flashing like an animated arrow just above the water. Or, if you are quiet and especially observant, you may come across one sitting motionless on a branch, concentrating fiercely on the canal below and intent on a fishy snack.

As in most parts of Britain, mammals are harder to observe than other wildlife although you are as likely to see foxes or hedgehogs here as anywhere else. But, because of the water, you might from time to time be lucky enough to hear the 'plop' and then watch the blunt whiskered nose of a water vole plying from one bank to the other. And where there are moorings and people, you are likely to find rats.

As was explained in the section dealing with the Wendover Arm, the Tring Reservoirs are as artificial in origin as the canal itself, but in the century-and-a-half since they were built they have taken on many of the characteristics of natural lakes. They are rich in wildlife and, after 1955, they were a National Nature Reserve managed by the Nature Conservancy Council. The Council, now English Nature, developed a nature trail almost 2 miles (3 km) long to enable wildlife enthusiasts to observe much of what the site has to offer. Control of the reservoirs reverted to British Waterways in 1989, and they are no longer a National Nature Reserve. British Waterways, however, continue to maintain the same high standards of habitat management to retain the diversity of the wildlife.

You are unlikely to see tufted ducks, pochard or shoveler on the canal but they are present on the reservoirs throughout the year. Between December and May, it is worth scanning the waters with binoculars to catch sight of the remarkable 'penguin dance' courtship ritual of the great crested grebes. In the reedbeds fringing Marsworth Reservoir there is a large colony of reed warblers, with sedge warblers in the nearby scrubland. These are not the only warblers present, and you should at least hear, if not see, chiff-chaffs, blackcaps and whitethroats. There is a public hide on Tringford Reservoir for the use of birdwatchers, and from there you might see wading birds such as sandpipers, redshanks, ringed plover, greenshank or even ruff.

This is only a small sample of the wide range of plants and animals you might chance upon if you follow the nature trail.

A Circular Walk to the Bridgewater Monument

3¾ miles (6 km). Allow 1½–2 hours

The walk begins from Bridge 135 to the east of Tring centre, on Station Road. Walk up the road towards Tring Station passing the Royal Hotel on your right. Pass by the little station and over the railway bridge. Although you have a roadwalk start to this journey, there is quite pleasant countryside all around. Where a road goes off to the left signposted to Ivinghoe and Pitstone, continue on bearing right towards Aldbury and Ringshall. By two dead trees, take the concrete farm road left which is signposted as a bridleway and bears the acorn symbol of the Ridgeway National Trail. Where the concrete way bends round to the left towards Westland Farm, your way goes straight on up a grassy track and you come to a wooden gate.

Go through the gate; do not turn left to follow the Ridgeway, but continue straight on up the bank towards another wooden gate and go through it. Follow the well-defined path across the field ahead towards a fence, a gate, and a hedgerow. Go through the gate and continue to follow the scrub-lined track. This is a bridleway and can be muddy and churned up after wet weather. It is lined with elders and blackthorn among other vegetation. There is lovely, rolling, partly wooded farmland all around, but there is also the noise of trains behind you. To your right you can see the village of Aldbury, with its square-towered church, tucked away in the valley beneath the wooded hills. As you pass the crossing of a footpath, the track begins to descend a little and then turns to the left. Hereabouts, in late summer, the red berries of dog roses adorn the bushes.

The bridleway then bears to the right and is rather broader, though still hemmed in on either side by high hedges so that it forms a shady, leafy, tunnel-like track. Mostly the going underfoot has become a little easier but there are some very boggy patches. Pass by a public footpath joining you from the left and continue on along the bridleway. There are some lovely blackthorn trees here which are heavy with sloes in late summer. There are blackberries and elderberries, too, so this is a very fruitful path. In places the blackthorns are so laden with fruit that they take on a ghostly bluish haze.

As you continue to descend gently, there are now grazing meadows for horses on your left and the track is very muddy and churned up again after rain. It soon becomes a partly metalled

The Bridgewater Monument.

lane, however, and there is a house and other buildings on your left. Where the lane reaches a narrow metalled road, turn left. After about a hundred yards of walking, look out on your right for a public footpath sign high up on the bank where there are some steps and the remains of a stile. Take this path heading towards the woodland on the ridge until you reach a stile on your left in the barbed wire fence beneath a sycamore tree. Cross the stile and head diagonally up the field on the righthand track.

Where the rather indistinct path forks, you take the righthand track up the hill, through the woods. This is a quite steep ascent. There is the occasional reassuring yellow arrow on the trees. This is a lung-testing but mercifully relatively short climb. By a red-brick and tile-hung house, you find another path crossing your way at an angle and you take this, bearing to the right and uphill again. This is at a signpost indicating that the way you have come is a footpath to Aldbury. Where you emerge on to a partially metalled lane, you turn right, still ascending but more gently this time, and soon you come to a tall column with its green patina-ed, decorative, urn-shaped top, set on the top of the hill in an open, grassy area. This is the Bridgewater Monument, part of the National Trust's Ashridge Estate, and any visitor may ascend the column for a fee at certain times of the day and year. The monument was erected in Honour of Francis the Third Duke of Bridgewater, 'Father of Inland Navigation', in 1832.

For the return journey from the monument follow the grassy track across the meadow towards the little cottage with a wooden fence, and at the end of the fence, there is a wooden garage and wooden outbuildings. On the metalled drive in front of Monument Cottage, turn right keeping its pretty garden and then the padlocked wooden garages on your left. Where the lane splits take the main track straight ahead descending the hill. Here there is a pleasant view down to Aldbury and the downs beyond and seats to help you enjoy it. The lane forks, and you bear right, descending the hill with pleasant glimpses of the village through the trees as you go down on the steepish chalky track. This soon becomes almost a gully and it could be slippery in wet weather. The track forks again but you carry on down the hill.

As you arrive in the village you come to some newly renovated cottages with Tudor-style chimneys and then to the Tom's Hill Road, where you bear right. You will come to the village centre with its pond and ivy-clad hotel. Continue straight on, following the signpost to Tring Station, 1 mile. This is a charming English village and, by the pond, there are some ancient stocks. Pass by the square-towered church of St John the Baptist at Aldbury. Follow the road back to Tring Station and your starting point. There are some sharp bends on this road and, although the rule usually is to walk on the right, before you get to some of these bends it may be safer to cross to the left. Although the roadside embankment is kept well trimmed, there are some attractive wild flowers to brighten the way.

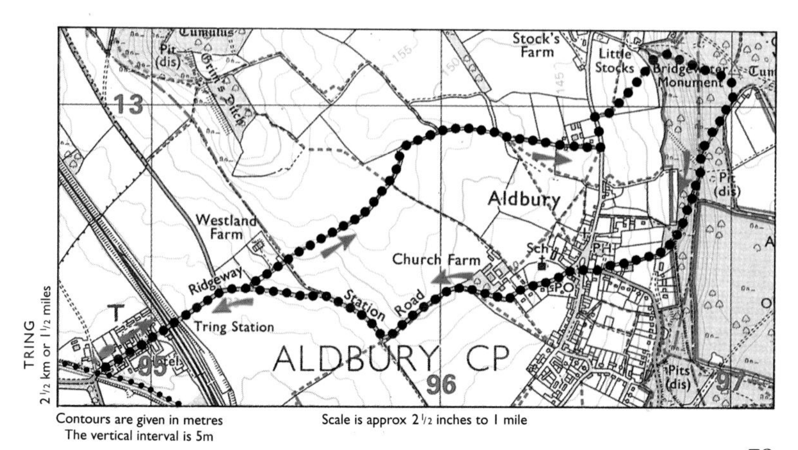

Contours are given in metres
The vertical interval is 5m

Scale is approx 2 1/2 inches to 1 mile

4

IVINGHOE TO FENNY STRATFORD

14 MILES (22 KM)

Pass beneath Bridge 123 with its iron reinforcing, dated 1913. The path ahead looks like a pleasant grassy way and, as you pass the golf driving range on your left, you still have Ivinghoe Beacon to your right. This is pleasant, rural walking across a plain so flat that one would have thought that there was hardly any need for locks, but you soon encounter Locks 33 and 32. The grassy path has cut a narrow swathe through a carpet of clover. Immediately past the first lock is the double-arched Bridge 122, and you also pass between electricity transmission towers. You soon pass by Lock 32 and the gradient is barely perceptible except by the lock itself. In fact you have descended a total of 14 feet 3 inches (4.25 metres) with the two locks. All around there is flat, open farmland, with surprisingly few grazing animals as we walked by. If you look closely at the occasional young willow sapling, you can see that the leaves are brightly dotted with bright red bumps like measles. These are galls caused by an infestation of parasitic insects. Look out, too, for the clumps of water dock, and you might see a watchful heron standing statue-like and staring intently into the water where a patch of weed conceals a likely meal of fish. A collection of farm buildings hard by Horton Lock (31) and Bridge 121 was presaged by an animal scent in the air. As we passed by, there were moored here an unkempt old narrow boat and a steel boat, its chimney capped by an old saucepan, and its stern guarded by a dog.

Pass beneath the towpath arch of the bridge, another ageing brick-built affair guarded by the stumps of two old trees which look as they have been struck by lightning. The path is soon grassy again. Now there are some stands of sedges by the water's edge where damselflies and speckled wood butterflies flit, and swallows weave. Just before you get to Bridge 120 the canal widens in a winding hole and then you are on to Slapton Lock with its white-painted cottage on the left and little chimneyed, brick-built pump house on the right. The grassy bank becomes rockier underfoot and the canal turns quite sharply to the right before bearing a little more gently left. Once again there are some fine stands of sedges where, after rain, the path might be a little muddy. Among the sedges was a chattering summer warbler and just the occasional angler enjoying the wildlife. Soon the path becomes grassy and there are young willows and more mature hawthorns along the banks.

There is no Bridge 119 but you soon come to the single iron girder span of Bridge 118. Supported on brick piers, it carries a farm track giving access from one field to another. The canal turns sharply right with a few white willow trees on the apex of the bend. The stillness of the countryside is broken only by the

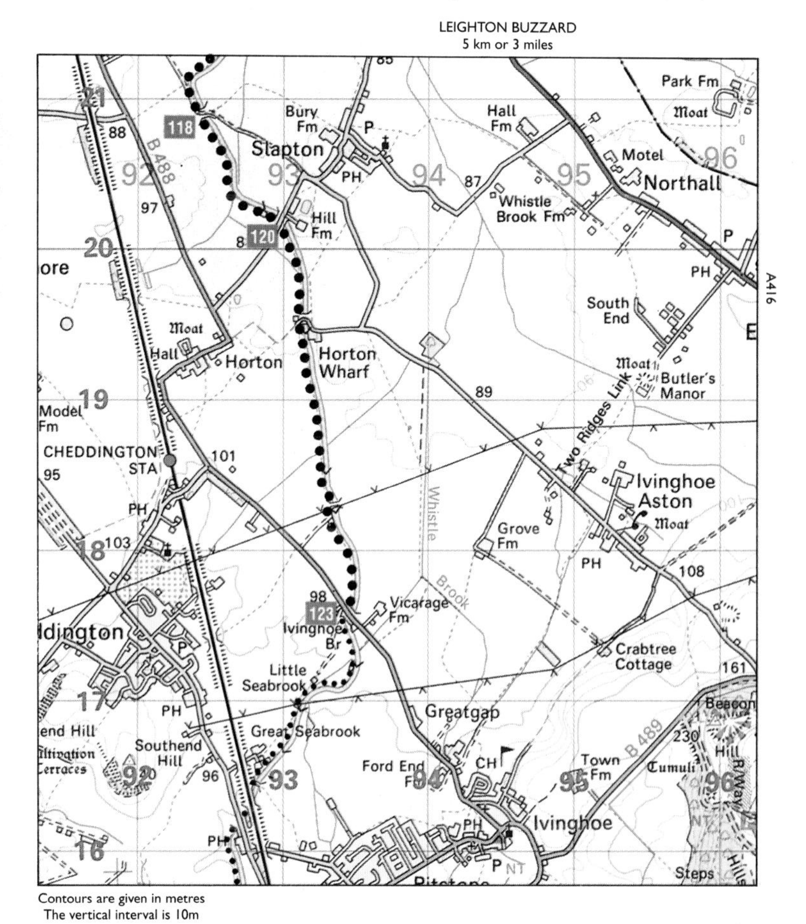

Contours are given in metres
The vertical interval is 10m

rushing of a passing train but tyre tracks in any muddy patches reveal that not only walkers use the towpath. The canal bends to the left again where more trees overhang the opposite bank and, in the late summer, fields of maize crowd down to the water's edge. There is no Bridge 117 but, before you reach Bridge 116, where the canal passes beneath overhead power cables, there is a little mixed deciduous woodland to your left. As well as sycamores and birch, the rowan trees are bright with their fecund clusters of orange-red berries at the end of summer.

Church Lock near Grove and Bridge 116 is named for its attractive little former church, now a private dwelling. It was the Church of St Michael and All Angels **(A)**, once the smallest church in Buckinghamshire, and served a small hamlet which lay in the fields across the lane. Grove was one of the smallest parishes in England and appears in the Domesday Survey. Cross Bridge 116 to continue along the path on the other bank, and on your right there is a paddock with practice jumps for horses. The noise of heavy traffic ahead gives warning of Leighton Buzzard and its busy bypass, but through it came the whistling call of a green sandpiper as it flew off low and fast, its white rump contrasting markedly with its near black-looking wings and body. And there are fragrant little patches of meadowsweet by the bank.

You soon come to Grove Lock, Number 28, with its usual lock-side white cottage; the rusting hulk, filled with marsh plants, of an old iron boat lay floundering by the lock as we passed through. The wild flowers here include mint, water forget-me-not, Himalayan balsam, white deadnettle and white comfrey. Pass beneath the ugly grey-white span of a bypass bridge, and the River Ouse joins you on the right, here much less impressive in scale than the canal. Some wooden piles, a bit of rotting wooden and iron pier, and a couple of sheds suggest that there must once have been a landing stage here on the left bank where beyond there are now some quite extensive reed beds. As you walk, look out for signs of trains on the towpath! Where the bank has a concrete quayside, you should find traces of old narrow-gauge tramways built in the 1920s to bring sand and gravel to the canal for onward transport by water. Most of the lines are overgrown or removed but the Leighton Buzzard Light Railway retains more than 3 miles of track as an attraction.

It is hard to believe that you are heading for the centre of Leighton Buzzard but the canal narrows and then widens again, presumably into a winding hole. The little River Ouse to your right is choked with aquatic weeds as well as the convolvulus trailing down to the water. Just as you are in sight of an old iron-girder bridge, there is a stadium on your left with its tall flood-lights, as well as a development of modern houses across the canal. Suddenly you have the spire of a church in Leighton Buzzard ahead to the right. Beyond the former railway bridge and the pipes that span the canal, there are some semi-detached modern houses on your left. Pass beneath a white-painted concrete and iron footbridge with its widely spaced steps to allow for wheelchairs and prams. With a playing field on your left, you are now approaching the heart of Leighton Buzzard. Debris and domestic ducks mark the proximity of 'civilization'. Pass by a little weir in the river on your right and there is a brickyard and various canal-side industries which probably no longer depend on the water for transport. As you begin to become hemmed in on either side by old and new brick, an arching bridge takes you over the entrance to an earlier canal dock, and there is a winding hole here. Pass by Leighton Linslade Sanitary Station before going under the concrete arch of Bridge 114. Close by, at Leighton Linslade Visitor Moorings, there is the *Lockside Bar and Waterside Terrace.*

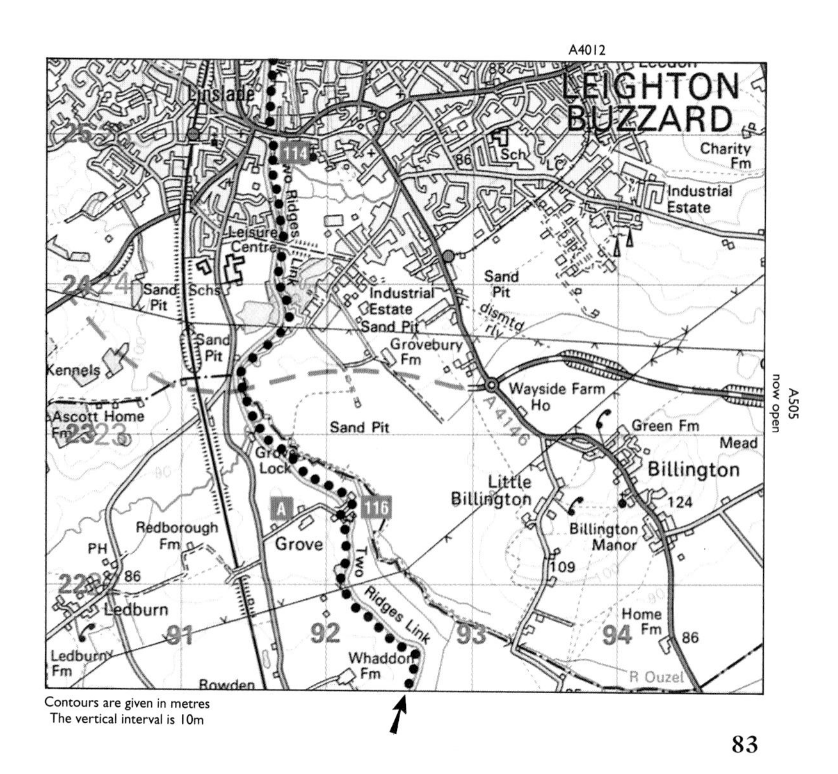

Contours are given in metres
The vertical interval is 10m

By a brick wall edging the towpath and a weir, a small river flows under the canal in a culvert. Beyond is the Wyvern Shipping hire boat base with a wet dock tucked away within an old orchard. You soon come to Leighton Lock prettily situated among the trees and well-kept gardens of waterside houses. Just before the lock is a newly roofed and rather odd-looking building with what would once have been stone-mullioned windows now filled in by ugly new mock-leaded windows. Leighton Buzzard is behind you and, just beyond the lock, the canal makes a sharp bend to the west before you come to Bridge 112, a former swing bridge, the remains of which may one day be rescued and restored. The trees all about make for pleasing and attractive walking. The canal is quite broad and rather river-like here, then suddenly there are the ugly structures which make up a sewage treatment plant – every town must have one! Soon, by Bridge 111, there is the garden and children's play area of the *Globe Inn*. Go beneath the gently arching iron bridge on its brick piers and continue along the towpath with its high bank to the left. The canal bends sharply to the right again immediately where the rail embankment is brick-supported. There are some mature willows here, bearing dark green clusters of mistletoe. Some trees are old and falling and, here and there, they have been cut back for safety reasons. On the left here are broad expanses of neatly trimmed sward, a church with castellated walls, and a seemingly low red-brick and stone manorial farm building which turns out to be Manor Farm, close by Bridge 110. This is Old Linslade, a deserted medieval village of which only the church and farm remain. As we passed through, a tiny brown wren flew, bullet-like, across the way. Just past the bridge, a vibrant border of orange marigolds and tall, round-faced sunflowers peer down to the water. There are gorse-clad banks on the left and pleasant, open meadowland with woods beyond, on the right.

The canal takes another sharp bend to the left and you are soon at Bridge 109. Pass beneath its crumbling brick arch with deeply scored rubbing bars, and there is the railway close by on your left. Suddenly we came upon a colourful clump of pale yellow common toadflax resembling garden snapdragons. And a great brown hawker dragonfly whirred out from the undergrowth. There are elderberries and hawthorns in abundance as well as bramble, dog rose, and, about 100 yards before Bridge 108, a fine clump of purple loosestrife. Though the road is close here, it is a pretty stretch of canal with hedges on either side and varied vegetation. Just before Bridge 107, there is a grassy area with picnic tables set out. You will need to cross to the other bank here. The bridge itself can be busy with traffic and, if you can, it is better to cross on the top lock gates of Soulbury Three Locks. Near by, there is the Three Locks Golf Club; the whole setting is most attractive with the rather commercialized *Three Locks Inn* attracting a thriving clientele. Look out here for signs of the former narrow duplicate locks.

Along the next stretch, the grassy path can be muddy after rain. The replacement concrete span of Bridge 106 takes you across the canal once again to continue on the right bank. This is the line of a public footpath and is also a metalled lane. The canal takes a turn to the left and then narrows between the remains of the derelict swing bridge, 105, which must once have linked the fields on either side. Soon come Lock 23 and Bridge 104 near Stoke Hammond, and the white-painted lock-keeper's cottage. Bridge 104 is double arched, and you walk beneath the landward arch. As we passed by, there were white Embden geese on the opposite bank and another heron lazily crossed the canal. Between the walker and the river on the right, there are little stands of *Phragmites* reeds.

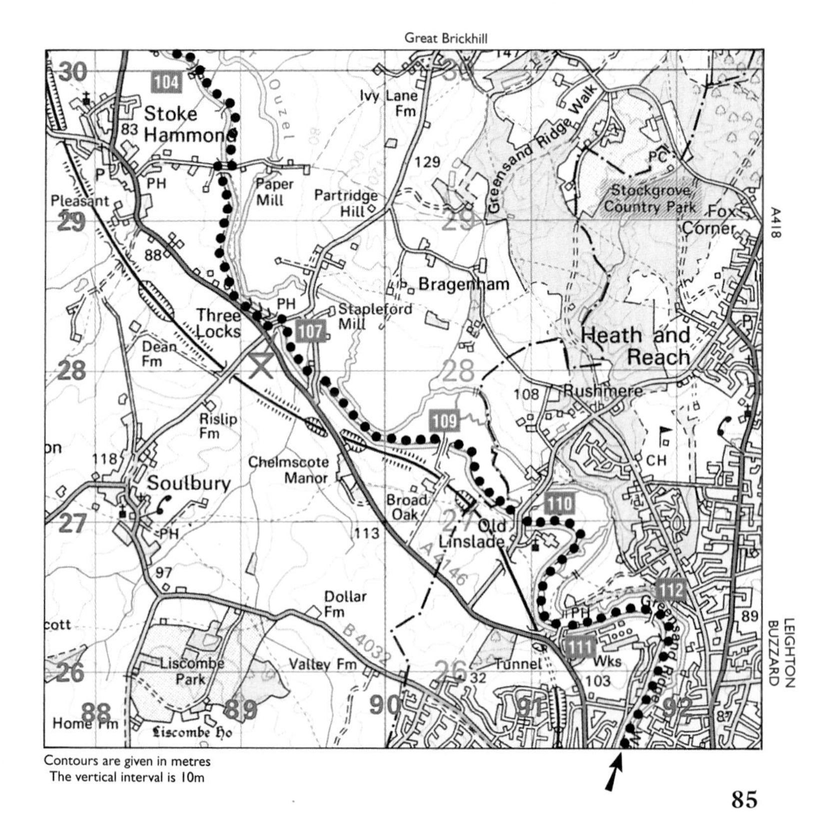

Pause for a pint: the Globe Inn at Linslade.

The Globe Inn A FREE HOUSE

The canal dipping down through the three locks at Soulbury on the way to Fenny Stratford.

The road is right next to the canal just before you reach Bridge 102, giving easy access for anglers, and here the towpath narrows a little. Carry on beneath the old brick arch. The canal now curves to the left and a familiar scent suggests the imminence of another sewage treatment works. Before you get to Bridge 99, mellowed with age, there are the facilities of Willow Bridge Marina, with a grocer's shop, chandlery and off-licence, and then a new concrete span. One of the boats here has been set up as a working pottery. A signpost tells you that you have come from Soulbury Three Locks and you are heading for Fenny Stratford. The towpath is now narrow but metalled and there is the noise of traffic all around. There is an avenue of poplars on your right with a hedge beyond. This is more urban walking with the hedgerows obviously regularly tended. Clearly, you are on the outskirts of Milton Keynes but, even here, there is the occasional neck-bobbing moorhen and there are green fields off to your right.

By the time you reach Bridge 98, you have passed some little, square, red-brick bungalows and equally pocket-sized gardens backing on to the canal. After the bridge, you have the outskirts of Bletchley, once a market town, now swallowed up by Milton Keynes as it has devoured Simpson beyond. The canal passes through a housing estate with an embankment disguising all but the roof tops on the left. Pass beneath the brick-built Bridge 97 and the similarly arching pipework. There are moorhens aplenty here upending and squabbling. Just before you get to Bridge 96, go over a little lifting bridge and there is a new concrete constructed marina on your right. Pass by red-brick offices and go under the bridge with the *Bridge Inn* on the lefthand side of the canal. Walk beneath another concrete and stone bridge with its flat single span and pipework in front, and then you come to Fenny Stratford Lock, 22, where there is the *Red Lion* on the lefthand side of the canal and there is also what looks like a swing bridge here. The pump house has been converted into a charity shop, closed as we passed by

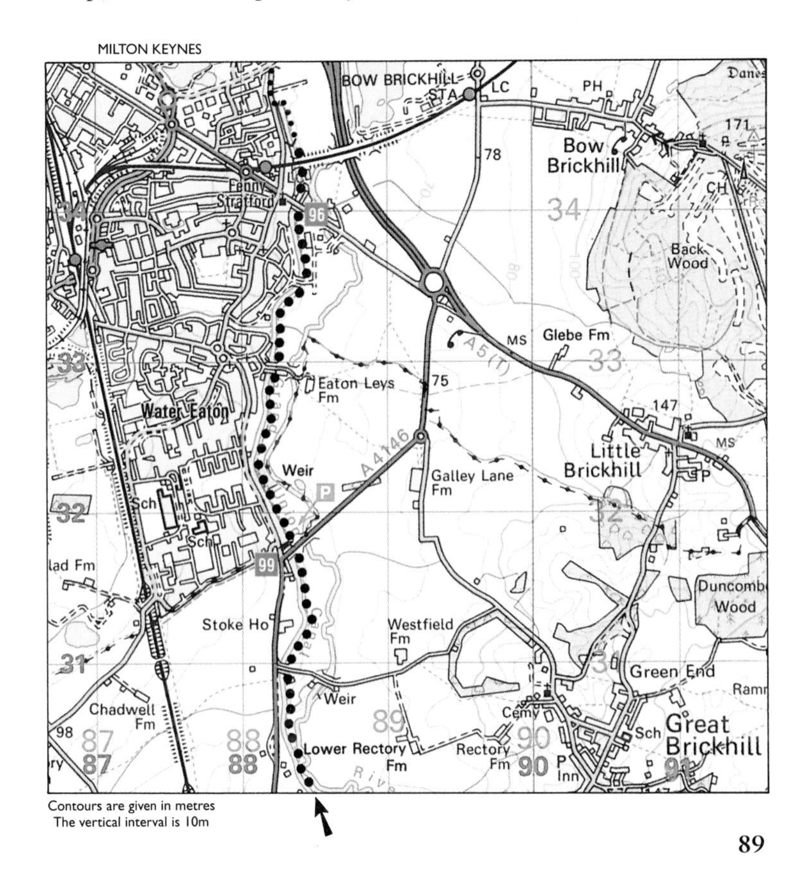

Contours are given in metres
The vertical interval is 10m

5
FENNY STRATFORD TO STOKE BRUERNE

17 MILES (27 KM)

Just beyond Fenny Lodge Gallery, look out for the house with its remarkably ornamented garden including a couple of gnomes standing atop two ivy-clad tree stumps. Ducks, both live and plaster of Paris, seem to be the theme here, however. Go under the newly built brick-and-concrete Bridge 94, beyond which are the factory buildings of, so we were told by a local dog walker, a company that manufactures flavouring essences which, on our day, seemed from the aroma to be blackberry jam. Pass beneath a new bridge carrying a road to Fenny Stratford. The next bridge is the brick-built 93, its nineteenth-century workaday charm contrasting with today's purely functional industrial buildings. As you pass beneath Bridge 92a, you cannot imagine that even with the mellowing of time, it will ever be anything but ugly, unlike its counterparts such as the old Bridge 92. Pass by a converted canal-side property and just beyond the seat, the canal makes a sharp turn to the left. Although you are accompanied by the constant noise of the road, and there are various developments here, the canal forms a pleasantly rural corridor through the built-up sprawl of greater Milton Keynes. As the canal bends to the right, you seem to be in a tree-sprinkled parkland. Pass by the canal-side garden of *The Plough* public house just before you get to Bridge 91, Bowlers Bridge.

Go under the new Bridge 90c, Groveway, where there is a parking area that is especially convenient for anglers. Lovely willows overhang the bank on the left now, while on the right there is another line of poplar trees. Go under a concrete and iron-railed footbridge leading from one landscaped stretch of parkland to another, and look out for the signs on either side indicating that the canal narrows here just before you get to Bridge 90, where again the new contrasts sharply with the old. The canal takes a

A modern city lays claim to a a traditional bridge.

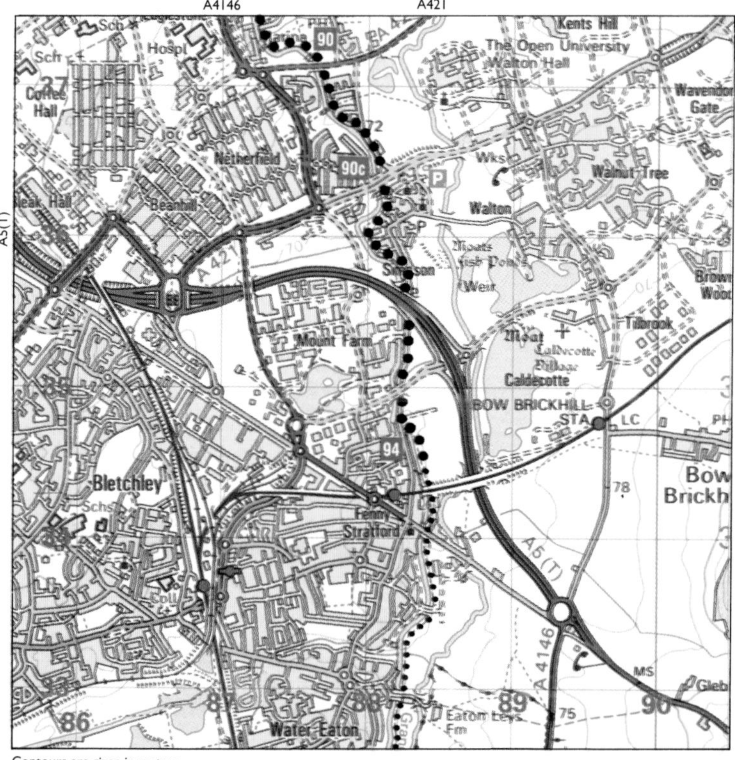

Contours are given in metres
The vertical interval is 10m

sharp bend to the left and there are mooring rings set in new concrete blocks. Pass beneath the solid-looking skew Bridge 89. On the opposite bank is the smart new Milton Keynes Marina where there are the usual facilities as well as a restaurant and bar, *The Moorings.* Go under Bridge 88, and horse chestnuts and elders overhang the bank. Round the bend you suddenly find yourself passing beneath Bridge 87, reinforced with steel tie bars.

Ahead, the canal resembles a river and there is a development of elongated blocks of flats to your left. The canal takes a bend to the left and there is the little iron-railed, brick-built Bridge 86 with its girder span. Landscaped meadowland and paddocks are to your right, with paling fences to separate the horses that graze there. Pass beneath Bridge 85a, built in 1983, carrying Saffron Way. Now there are the steeply roofed, red-brick, red-tiled, black-balconied modern terraces of a new development on your left. The communal gardens have been well landscaped to blend with the rural feel of the canal. Go under Bridge 85, and at Bridge 84 the engineering bricks from which it is made claim their date as 1910 while the bridge itself is dated 1937 – it still bears its partly worn rubbing bars showing that horse-drawn boats have passed beneath it. Round a lefthand bend is the brick-built Bridge 83; the towpath becomes rather narrow here. Dead ahead now you can see the ugly concrete span of Bridge 82a carrying Child's Way.

Pass beneath Bridge 82a and continue following the towpath, which is now partly gravelled. Just before Bridge 82 there is a winding hole and by the bridge itself a seat where there is a signpost pointing to Pennyland ahead and Springfield behind. Just ahead now is another new bridge built from brick, concrete and steel with a line of poplar trees beyond. In the field to your left, near Bridge 81b, is a slightly odd, reddish-coloured steel or concrete sculpture which, at certain angles, resembles a cut-out head. Here, in late summer, wild roses dot the bank with their orange-red hips. Go under another large concrete skew span just before you reach a housing estate on the left bank. Beneath the bridge the way is tiled, and, while the towpath sticks to the canal, running parallel to it on your right is a gravel track in an avenue of poplar trees. Beneath an overhanging willow, there is another new bench – one of several along the way – and on your left the balconied houses stand proudly in red brick. The path becomes narower, hemmed in by hedge and monk's rhubarb and then there is a children's play area on the opposite bank as you approach Bridge 81. Although you are walking through the heart of Milton Keynes, the towpath is immaculately kept, thanks to the efficient housekeeping of the local authority.

Go under Bridge 81 and the canal is guarded by mature hawthorns, willows, ash and more. It is a popular path for dog-walkers. Go under the new, brick-piered, wooden-balustraded Bridge 80a and, although you are passing through a housing development, it is attractive easy walking and everything about you is neatly trimmed and well kept. Bridge 79d is soon followed by Pennylands, a prestige development where occupiers of the waterside red-brick houses have the advantage of being able to keep their boats right outside their back doors in a private basin.

The canal begins to make a bend to the left, westwards, as another new concrete and iron footbridge comes into view. Pass beneath its span and the neatly cut grass banks on the opposite side, mature hawthorn hedges on your right, and fine planted willow trees to the left make for pleasant walking. Pass beneath another grey-railed, concrete and brick-built footbridge. Soon after comes Bridge 79a carrying the A422, Monks Way. Here the

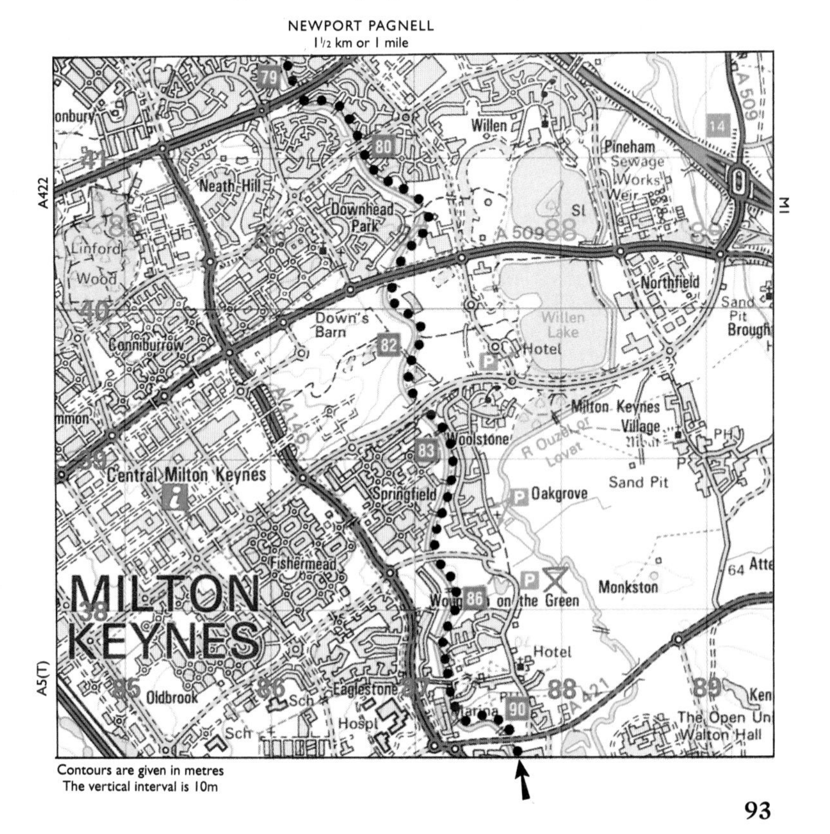

towpath seems rather to disappear but you just continue along the grass verge at the water's edge. Walk by a sizeable mooring for boats, the Lion Hearts Cruising Club, and you are soon passing beneath the old brick and concrete arch of Bridge 79. Once again, ahead of you, there is a line of poplar trees and the towpath becomes partly metalled. Look out for the restored brick kilns on the opposite side; coal delivered by boat was used to fire the bricks for the Wolverton Railway Workshops.

Pass beneath Bridge 78, an old brick-piered affair. It was due to be demolished as part of the Milton Keynes masterplan so it does not appear on Ordnance Survey maps. Local people protested, however, and new, wooden decking was added to the half-demolished bridge. Then follows the new canal-side pub, *The Giffard Park*. The going underfoot is roughly metalled and the canal swings westwards. Pass by another new, landscaped housing development on your right. Ahead looms Bridge 77.

Pass by the refurbished Old Wharf House, and there is a winding hole here as well as a Grand Junction Canal Trail information board. This is at Linford Wharf **(A)**. Note that the Newport Pagnell Canal joined the Grand Junction Canal ten yards west of here. It went out through what is now a workshop with blue doors and descended through seven locks to Newport Pagnell 1¼ miles away. This arm was closed in 1864. There are various circular walk possibilities here and a fine buddleia tree. Bridge 77 was constructed in 1913 and, immediately beyond it, there is a steel footbridge. There are more houses, new and old, to your right and the landscaped parkland continues on your left.

Pass by the square-towered church of Great Linford on the far bank hiding among beautifully kept trees and, on the opposite bank, there are walks, benches and picnic tables again. Go on under Bridge 76a, crossing the canal askew, and walk by the garden and play area of the *Black Horse* pub near the newly rebuilt Black Horse Bridge, 76. The towpath becomes a narrow, tarmacked lane and the canal bends a little to the left. The lane then veers to the right, where there is a cattle grid, and it is signposted as a public bridleway, Swan's Way, a long-distance route from the Thames to Salcey Forest, and there are the extensive flooded gravel workings which form the Wildfowl Centre at Great Linford Pits **(B)**.

You have now left Milton Keynes behind you and you are into pleasant open farmland where, in the water, old willows have created miniature islands for themselves, stranded, perhaps as the bank was undercut behind them. The spike of a chimney just pokes above the top of a low hill on the immediate horizon ahead, seemingly just to the left of Bridge 75, an old brick structure now carrying nothing but a track. Shortly afterwards, the canal takes a turn left, southwards, before veering westwards again towards New Bradwell. On the apex of the bend is a weir draining off to the right, and the meadow to the left is pitted with hollows. Although the surroundings are rural, the towpath is still metalled and the gravel pits to the right come closer, with the development of Wolverton beyond.

You are approaching New Bradwell where Bridge 74 is a brick, concrete, and iron-railed affair. Soon red- and orange-brick, modern detached houses gaze over the canal and some have little jetties with narrow boats tied alongside. Pass beneath Bridge 72 and note that, on the other side, there is the *New Inn* offering lunches and evening meals. Near by is the eighteenth-century stone tower windmill, with cap and sails restored. Pass by a little winding hole before the canal is contained and railed in a modern aqueduct going over the busy V6 dual carriageway on the outskirts of Milton Keynes. Here a weir drains the canal off down to the right into a tributary of the River Great Ouse. Then the battered concrete edges of the canal proclaim their building in 1934 while on the right there are several clusters of teasels. Ahead there is the swish and roar of the railway.

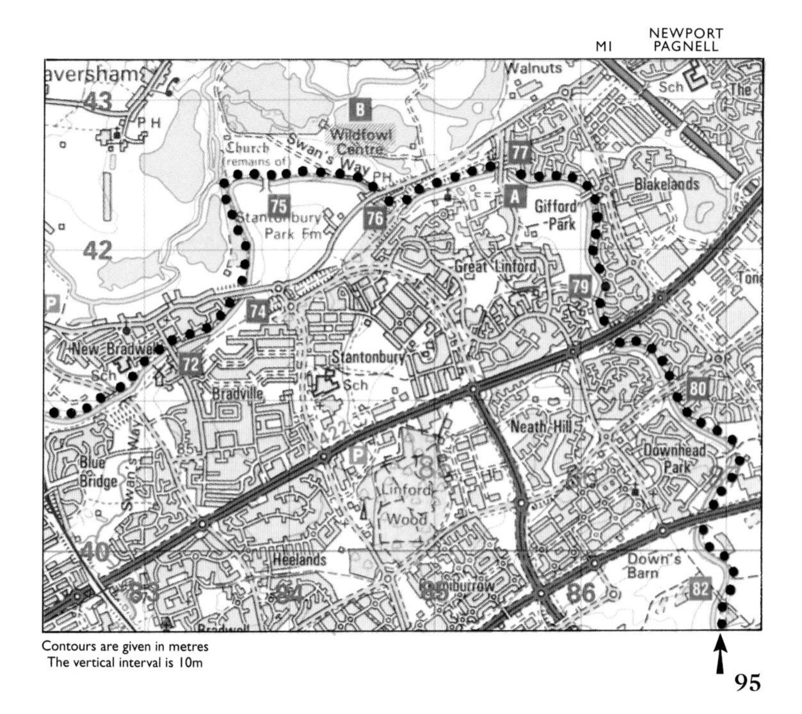

Contours are given in metres
The vertical interval is 10m

Soon the canal joins the railway and passes beneath it. Then a splendid mural of an unlikely train decorates the white-painted brick bank opposite (**C**). All mixed up in the train are blimps, helicopters, transporter tanks, veteran cars and biplanes, and there are locomotives from different eras at either end. Overhanging the towpath are weeping willows and hawthorns, and there is a short line of horse chestnuts before you reach the sturdy brick and concrete Bridge 71 where there is an information board for Wolverton. Victorian-looking industrial buildings glower down redly on to the canal. Next comes Bridge 69b and shortly after yet another bridge and, looking somewhat out of place, nestling in a patch of grass between the two, a little picnic table.

Now the footpath is tarmacked and there are high rambling brambles clambering over the trees. Pass beneath the ivy-clad Bridge 69 and the canal becomes a leafy tunnel with Braunston apparently 28 miles away. Ahead is the newly built Bridge 68 and right by the bridge is *The Galleon* public house. After the building supplies yard, the canal passes through more attractive park-like countryside.

The Iron Trunk Aqueduct (**D**) – a scheduled Ancient Monument – carries the canal over the River Great Ouse, flowing prettily far below through willow-decked meadows and fields. Note here the wide expanse of water, a reminder that, until 1805, the canal descended through four locks to the river which boats would cross before rising by similar locks on the north side. The information board describes the details. There is a pleasant walk under the canal just before the aqueduct from which you can get a good view of the structure. To the right there is a flooded burrow pit which was used to provide the material to build the canal's embankment. From here the North Bucks Way and the Grafton Way – two important regional walking routes – head south to the Chilterns and north to Badby respectively. You soon come to a lock, Cosgrove Lock. Beyond it the old Stratford Arm disappears to the left, leading in turn to the Buckingham Branch after 1 ½ miles. Sand and gravel were quarried to the east of Cosgrove, down among the caravan park; a narrow-gauge tramway brought the materials to the canal side, but the rails in the concrete are the only reminders. Soon, on the opposite bank, the lawn of the *Barley Mow* pub sweeps down to the canal. Ahead is Bridge 65, built of newly cleaned and repaired Northamptonshire stone, finely decorated and known as Solomon's Bridge (**E**). It is carved and boasts an elegant, almost

Moorish, arch. Cross here to the other side of the canal. It is only from the canal that you can appreciate this bridge, and look out for the plaque, too.

The towpath is now a gravelly way and there is tree-peppered meadowland on your right with a high hedge on your immediate left. The canal makes a series of bends here and is reinforced with new steel piling. Look out to the horizon to the right for the curious round tower – a water tower that supplied the nearby railway troughs used by steam locomotives to pick up water at speed. Pass by another weir draining the canal on your right. You soon arrive at more well-kept moorings and the newly rebuilt Bridge 64 at Thrupp or Castlethorpe Wharf where there is *The Navigation* pub. Cross to the right bank again. The track is now a dirt towpath and there is arable land to your left.

The canal makes a bend to the right and the towpath becomes a pleasant grassy way. Through breaks in the trees, you can see good, rich, flat farmland to right and left. Where the canal takes a turn to the left, look out for the derelict buildings on the left and just here is the brick arch of Bridge 63 with its deeply worn rubbing bar. Off to the right you will notice the prominent spire of

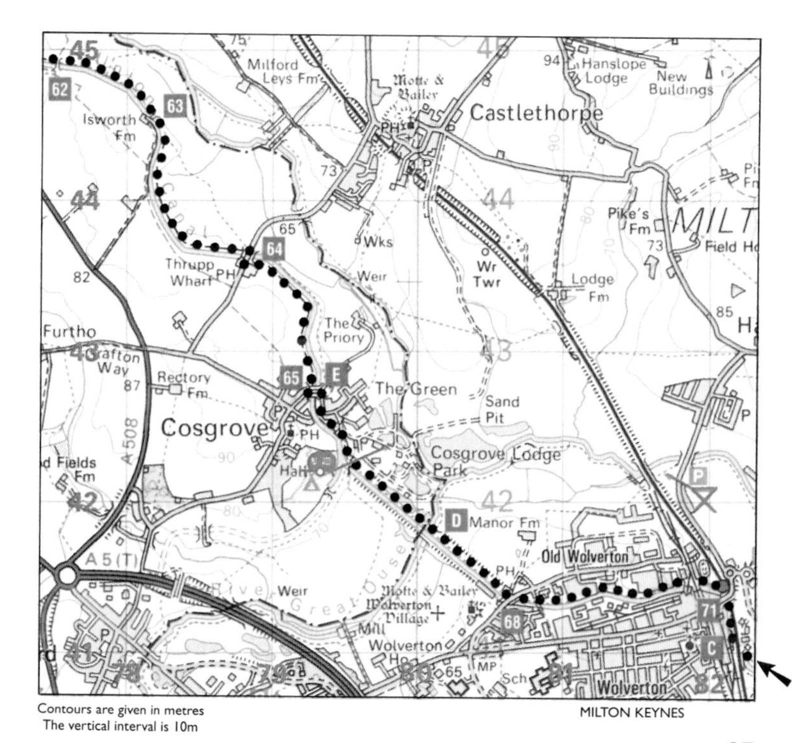

Contours are given in metres
The vertical interval is 10m

MILTON KEYNES

Hanslope church. Look out for the red (when unopened), cigar-shaped clusters of redshank flowers among the plant's spear-shaped leaves. There are also the little yellow flowers of black medick among the grass. Pass beneath the gently curving iron arch of Bridge 62 and the going ahead gets a little rougher. To your left you can see the little church spire of Yardley Gobion and the gentle iron arch of Bridge 61 looms up. A sign tells you that Yardley Wharf is ahead, and you now have the busy A508 to your left. The line of anglers and moored boats heralds the arrival of Bridge 60 and the wharf with its winding hole. The marina flies the White Ensign as well as the Union Flag. There is a dry dock here, too.

The path is narrow and bramble edged with broken banks and muddy patches. At Bridge 59 dating from 1934, the canal makes a bend to the right, and ahead on the hill is the square church tower of Grafton Regis. Bridge 58 comes into view in the distance. Where the canal makes a bend to the left, the towpath goes over a nine-arched, brick-walled weir draining to the River Tove on the right. The going underfoot soon becomes easier again and the canal then curves to the left. On the left bank are some old, gnarled, pollarded willows and you soon arrive at Bridge 57 giving access to Grafton Regis to the left. As we paused by the bridge, it carried a huge combine harvester above the water.

The canal bends to the right and the towpath continues with arable farmland all around. Bridge 56 is in sight and, as we passed, a heron heaved heavily skywards. At the bridge the canal bears left and on the outside curve large engineering bricks reinforce the bank to prevent erosion. To your left you can still see the sturdy church tower of Grafton Regis; shortly you come to another overflow weir, this time fenced, and there are the candy-striped pink and white flowers of lesser bindweed. Then there is a blackthorn and elder hedge. At the end of another weir there is a pair of rough-trunked old willows. You soon come to the first of the seven Stoke Bruerne locks with its little brick-built, chimney-potted pump-house dating from 1939. Walkers may use either side although the righthand route has limited headroom under the bridge ahead, and the grass is kept longer to encourage small mammals. The lefthand path is lovely, comfortable grass. Go under the ugly concrete bridge carrying the A508 and the path is ridged with engineering bricks to give the horses extra purchase – not so comfortable for the walker. Immediately after the bridge comes the next lock followed by two more in quick succession. The seven locks raise the canal a mere 40 feet (12 metres). Pass by the former lock-keeper's cottage at the last of the main flight and, beyond the pool at the back of the cottage, an old barrel has been used as a dovecote. Ahead, perched on a hill, you can see the square church tower of Stoke Bruerne. Rise up by Lock 15 and then comes the double-arched Bridge 53; walkers on the left bank must cross to the right here, either across the lock gates or over the bridge itself. On the left bank, the *Boat Inn* retains some of the old boating charm while, opposite, the Bruerne's Lock restaurant and the Old Chapel Tearooms cater for good appetites. The main attraction of Stoke Bruerne, however, is the Canal Museum providing a wonderful insight into the history of England's canals and the social demands of life afloat. The Museum Shop **(F)** also boasts a large range of canal-related books. Stoke Bruerne can be a very popular tourist spot, especially in summer.

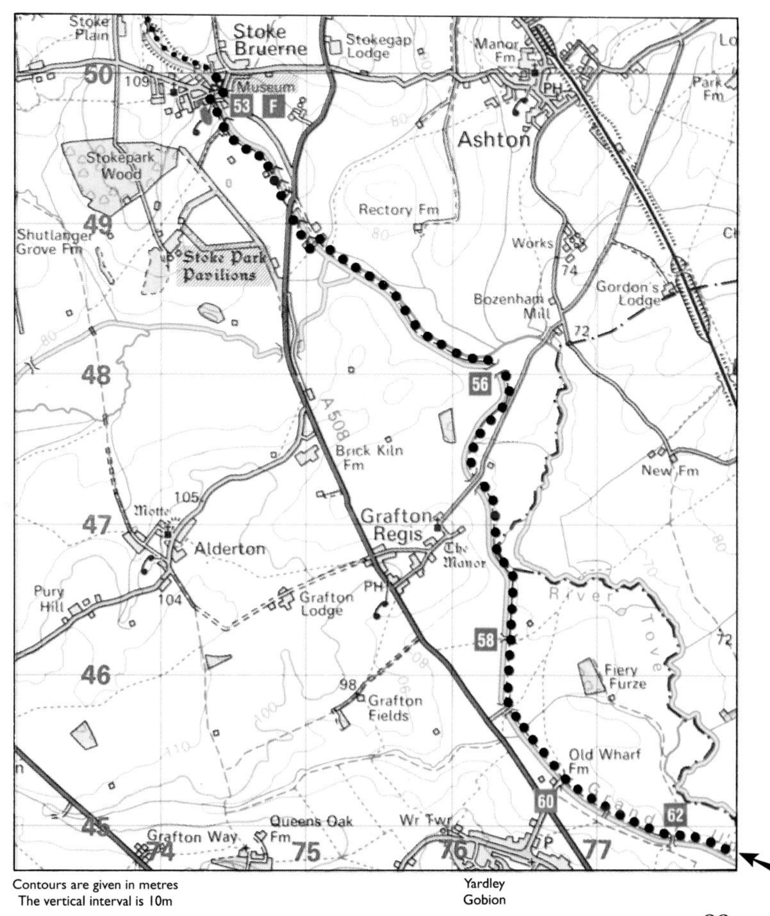

Contours are given in metres
The vertical interval is 10m

Yardley Gobion

A Circular Walk from New Bradwell

6¼ miles (10 km)

The walk begins on the canal towpath at Bridge 72 (1). Follow the path to the east – the canal will be on your righthand side – for approximately a mile and a half. The walk begins by skirting New Bradwell, a new town built to house workers at the Wolverton works of the London and Birmingham Railway. By Bridge 74 the walk enters open country. Beyond Bridge 75, a short way past the mile post indicating Braunston 31 miles, turn left through the iron gates (2) on to the metalled track that runs back at an acute angle. The track leads down to flooded gravel workings and swings round to pass the ruins of the twelfth-century Church of St Peter, former parish church of Stantonbury **(A)**. There is evidence of a number of houses around it, but the village centre is now to the north – probably removed when Stantonbury Park was created. The path swings round to the right – the lake to the left is used for water sports, separated from the lake to the right, a waterfowl sanctuary, by the meandering Great Ouse. Cross the river at the bridge by the weir (3). Beyond that is a mill stream and the mill, which has lost its waterwheel, though the sluices can still be seen. Immediately past the mill (4) turn right in the direction indicated by the 'Public Footpath' sign in the field. At the top of the rise (5), turn left towards the stile and head towards the lake. Continue across the field to the stile opposite and then walk towards the small conifer plantation and go through the gate between the edge of the plantation and the lake. Follow the edge of the lake round, continue on along the narrow neck of land between the two lakes, then turn slightly right to join the road by the two tall gateposts (6).

At the road turn right. The road crosses the river on an attractive brick bridge. Immediately before the Newport Pagnell sign (7) turn right on to the signposted bridleway and footpath. At the end of the bridleway (8) cross straight over the road and continue on to Great Linford. At the end of the row of houses (9) turn left down the slope which brings you to the platform of the former Great Linford station, on the short Newport Pagnell branch line of the London and Birmingham Railway. The line was closed in 1964 and has now been given a new surface for use as a cycleway and footpath. Turn right on to the path. It crosses the canal on a girder bridge, and after just over a mile

New Bradwell windmill appears up ahead, a stone tower mill with boat cap and four sails, now restored **(B)**. Leave the track by the bridge before the windmill, the site of New Bradwell station (10) and turn right to return to the start. To visit the windmill turn left and follow the signs on the opposite side of the road.

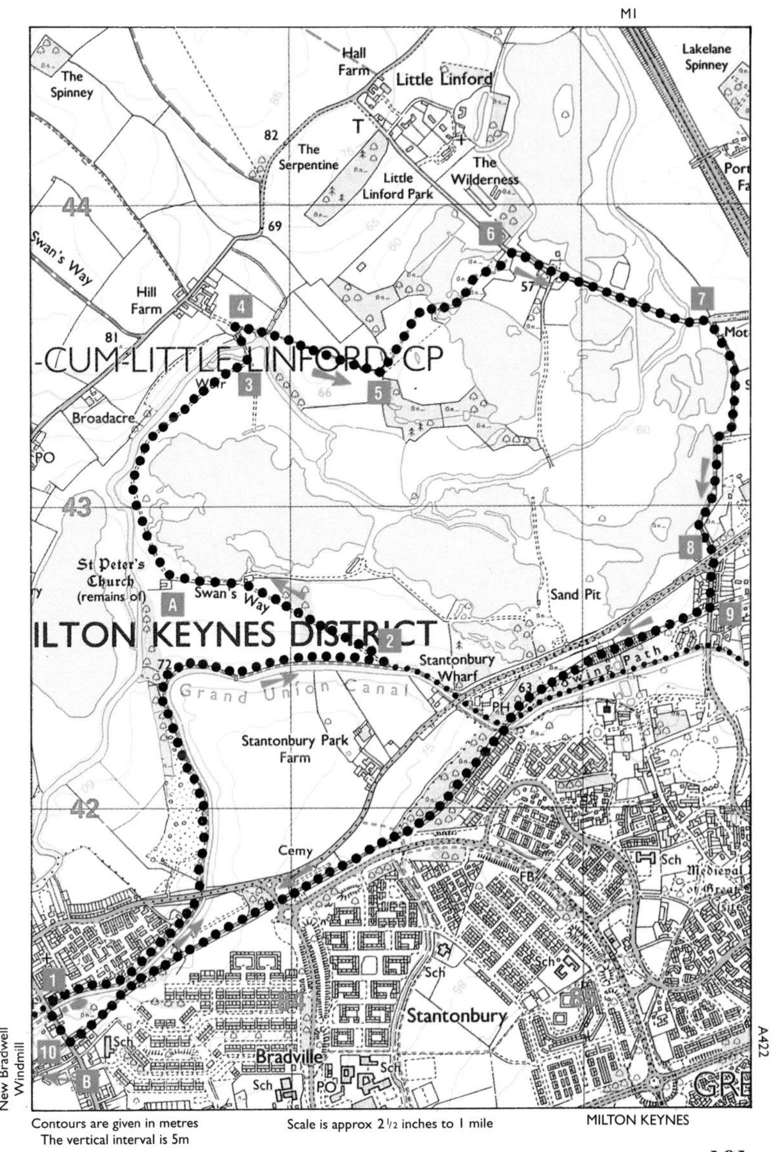

A Circular Walk from Stoke Bruerne

3 miles (5 km). Allow 1½ hours

A good starting point for this walk is the Canal Museum at Stoke Bruerne, just to the north of Bridge 53. There is a pay and display car park behind the museum.

From the museum, cross the canal by the lock gate towards the *Boat Inn*. From the inn, walk towards the bridge, passing the boat weighing machine on your left. As you arrive at the road by the bridge, look out on the opposite side of the road for a public footpath signpost to Alderton. This is by Waterways Cottage. Go through the farm entrance gate and bear to the left along a broad track which is gravelled at first. This track parallels the canal for a hundred yards or so before it bears to the right. Shortly after, there is a reassuring black arrow on a white circle indicating a public footpath. You will have these markers to follow throughout the route. Carry on straight ahead between a trimmed hedge on the right and a rather older, wilder row of shrubbery to your left. To your right, you can see the square-towered church of St Mary's looking down on the village. You are now walking along a broad, green lane. To your left is a disused brickworks, in operation between 1849 and 1920, but now a nature reserve. Look out for the peppering of little, grassy hillocks.

Ahead now, stretching stiffly skywards, is a stand of old poplars. The hedge on your left soon turns away to reveal a broad open field. Go through a narrow iron gate and continue walking through what you will have now realized is an avenue of poplars; it marks the former drive to Stoke Park House. Where the main track seems to bear to the left towards the farm buildings, continue straight on keeping a wire fence on your immediate right, and look out for a footpath marker on an old poplar directing you up the slope. To your right, there is an ancient oak. Initially, you should be aiming at a telegraph post on which you can just make out in the distance another footpath arrow. On the right, beyond the wire fence, there is a free-range chicken farm. When you reach the telegraph post, simply follow the direction of the arrow, and in the fields to your right, you will notice the ridge and furrow.

A few yards to the left of another old broken oak tree, look out for the footpath arrow on an old stile crossing an iron fence. Go over the stile, and bear a little to the right as shown. Ahead, on a small tree by a wooden fence there is another arrow to

The undisturbed charm of Great Linford.

draw you onwards towards the next stile. Climb the stile on to the farm track which takes you on to a metalled lane. Cross the lane and go through the gate on to another farm track. There is then another gate in an iron fence and, on the post by the gate ahead, there is a footpath arrow. Go through this gate and follow the direction of the arrow, initially keeping the line of the fence on your immediate left but heading towards the open gate down the hill ahead. You are walking through pleasant grazing meadows where there is more evidence of ridge and furrow. Walk through the next gate and then the right of way veers a little to the right which, as we walked through, was marked by a line of slender wooden stakes. As you descend the hill, towards a forking ivy-clad tree, you can just see the footpath arrow ahead of you. Here, you cross the line of a gully on a brick bridge. Follow the clearly defined path towards a wooden gate where there is another footpath arrow. Cross another little stream by a brick bridge.

At the gate, go over the stile and turn right on to what is now a public bridleway along the edge of a large, open field with a high hedge with standards to your immediate right. After about 300 yards, pass by a mature holly tree and ahead there is a waymarked hunting gate which you pass through. Carry on straight ahead, following the line of the trees on your right. Here and there, some of the larger trees have reassuring white arrows painted on them. Pass by a multi-stemmed old willow in the curve of a meander, keeping the stream to your right. Ahead and to the left in the distance, by another ivy-draped tree, you can make out another waymark at a hunting gate. Go through the gate and carry on along the public bridleway, initially keeping the stream on your immediate right.

Where the stream takes a sharp bend to the right, look out for an old, broken tree just beyond the low ridge ahead and a little to the left; it bears a white-painted arrow. Head towards the tree, which is also to the immediate right of transmission towers. You are now heading across the field. Bear a little further left towards an iron gate where there is an old wooden footbridge. Cross the bridge and you can now see the waymark on the tree quite clearly. Follow the line of the path as indicated by the arrow, and ahead in the distance, just before the buildings of Shutlanger, you should be able to make out what seems to be another white way marker. Aim

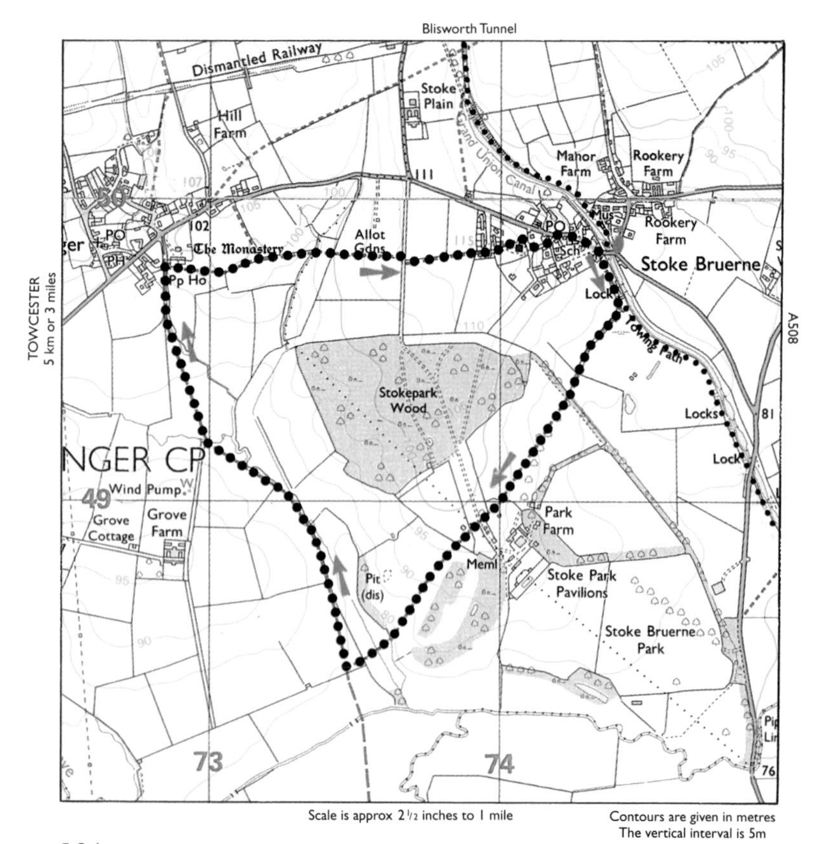

Scale is approx 2 1/2 inches to 1 mile

Contours are given in metres
The vertical interval is 5m

for it, but look out for more evidence of ridge and furrow. On the hill a little to the right of Shutlanger village, you can see the monastery with its thirteenth-century porch facing the footpath.

At the end of the field, you come to an iron farm gate with a wooden hunting gate next to it where there is indeed a waymark. But the white mark that you saw from the distance turns out to be the back of a sign 'This Land is Private Property' Take note of its content. You come out on to Water Lane and you carry on up the lane where there is a big, modern, yellow-brick, almost ranch-style bungalow on your left, and there are landscaped gardens with a rockery in front of it. Beyond the bungalow, and immediately by quite an elegant, square, stone-built Georgian house, look out on the right for a public footpath signpost (to Stoke Bruerne) which takes you through a gate, and you have the old walls of the monastery on your immediate left.

Follow the line of the track, which is broad at first, up the slope towards a farm gate in a hedge ahead. As you reach the gate, look out for the footpath sign on the telegraph post pointing you along the line of the hedgerow, and then you can see the waymarked stile in the botom corner of the field ahead. Cross the stile, and carry on keeping the hedge on your left this time and you are aiming for a white waymark on the tree ahead in the corner of the field. At the waymark, go over the stile and across a narrow, wooden footbridge. Go up the hill on the clearly defined footpath and you come to another stile in an old hedge. Cross the stile and continue on, gently uphill, keeping the wire fence to your right. Ahead you can just see the fifteenth-century upper parts of Stoke Bruerne church. Go over another stile on to a metalled lane.

Turn right on to the lane and almost immediately left through a gap in the hedge. Follow the path along the edge of the field aiming towards the church. Pass by a recreation field on your left, and just by a pale brick bungalow, you cross another waymarked stile on to a tarmacked footpath among houses. Pass by the end of a *cul-de-sac* on your left and head towards the church. Instead of going through the church gate, however, you take the public footpath through the remains of a kissing gate on the left. Follow the line of the boundary fence of the church down the slope towards a footpath waymark at the bottom of the field. At the waymark, bear right and then, after just a few yards, at a corner of the fence, bear to the left again. Soon you come to a stile in a neatly laid hedge. Go over the stile, bear left along the raised footpath down the lane. Turn right into Baker's Lane and you soon find yourself back at the *Boat Inn* in Stoke Bruerne.

6
Stoke Bruerne to Lower Weedon

12 MILES (19 KM)

From Stoke Bruerne, continue on the tarmacked towpath on the righthand side of the canal, passing a winding hole before you reach the entrance to the Blisworth Tunnel **(A)**. Just before you get to the tunnel, a track leads you up the hill to the right and walkers must leave the canal here for there is no towpath through the tunnel. There are moorings here as well as engineering brick ridges to enable horses to gain more purchase – perhaps to help them get their loads moving after the boats emerged from the tunnel. Boats would have been 'legged' through by the boatmen together with a specially hired legger using his own legging board. This lasted until 1871 when a steam tug was introduced which continued in service until 1936, by which time there were enough motor boats around to render the tug obsolete. A plaque commemorates the re-opening of the tunnel in 1984; a segment of the rebuilt tunnel is on display by the canal's right bank. The new circular tunnel (the old one was almost oval) is made from separate segments of concrete which, when linked together, form the complete ring-sections.

Look out at the top of the ramp for a terrace on the right. This is the course of the Blisworth Hill Tramway, a narrow-gauge, horse-drawn route used to connect the completed ends of the canal before the tunnel was opened in 1805. Continue to follow the leafy lane, and pass between the still-standing brick piers of the bridge which once carried the railway later known as the 'Banana Line' because it linked the major fruit ports of South Wales with the produce markets of East London. Then the lane bears to the left and rises gradually. Where you reach the minor road, you bear right, effectively straight on, towards the squat-looking tower-like structure beside a small collection of buildings which is the second of the ventilation shafts for the tunnel. Indeed, the road follows the line of the Blisworth Tunnel which is now on your left, and the brick-built chimney-like ventilation shafts on your left serve as poignant reminders of the boats plying through the tunnel, and the tremendous efforts the leggers must have made to keep their 30-ton loads on the move. You are, in fact, following the tunnel horsepath; the horses would have been walked over the tunnel by the children. Pass by the nicely named Buttermilk Hall Farm on your left and then there is a Camping and Caravanning Club Site. Pass by, on your right, the newly built stone walls of Southern Wood and follow a neatly kept hedge on your left. Go on past an entrance to Blisworth Hill Farm and you are now close to the summit of Blisworth Hill. By the entrance to the farm, there is another ventilation shaft, one of seven still showing. After 100 metres or so of level walking, the way starts to go gently down hill. Pass by the gate to Tunnel Hill Farm on your left and soon another minor road joins you from the right. This is signposted to 'Roade' but your way continues on, signposted towards Blisworth. Immediately on your left is another ventilation shaft. Pass the solid-looking Tunnel Hill House on your right and Blisworth itself comes into view ahead. Just before you reach the attractive, perhaps Georgian, stone-built and slate-roofed house bearing the unlikely appellation of Blisworth Stone Works, look out for the bridleway on your left. Take this and then, almost immediately, turn right to go down a concrete track to the canal.

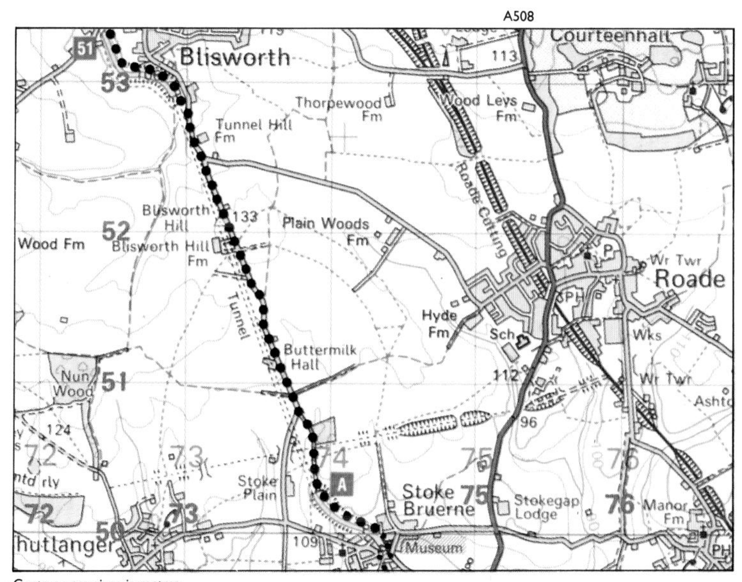

Contours are given in metres
The vertical interval is 10m

Behind you, as you join the canal again in a pleasant, leafy cutting, you can see the entrance to the tunnel. There is a sluice feeding the canal on your left. The path then becomes a little muddy after wet weather and is somewhat uneven at first. Once again, the canal is quite river-like with trees overhanging it on both sides. Moored boats herald the approach of Bridge 51 in Blisworth. Go under the bridge and hard by it is the solid-looking red-brick building of Westley Mill, dated 1879, with its now blinded, broken, and bricked-up windows and entrances. The heavily altered building next door, with canopy still intact, was a trans-shipment shed built in 1801 and owned by Pickfords. It was used to transfer goods from boats to the tramway. Bridge 51 has an extra brick and concrete span apart from the old brick arch which still has its rubbing bars. There was once direct access to the canal from the Mill, indicating that it must have made use of water transport for its products. Pass by the Canal Shop and Blisworth Tunnel Boats Limited on your left, and the little back gardens of several canal-side houses approach the water, and there is also a little grazing paddock on the left. Dog owners here are advised to keep their charges on a lead. Go over the concrete path by the drainage weir close to Bridge 50 and on beneath the bridge. Now to your left you have an open, arable hill.

The canal bears to the left and Bridge 49 soon comes into view. Pass beneath its single span of dark new bricks and concrete and, on your left, there is a sign pointing out the *Blisworth Hotel.* Next comes a railway bridge with its blue-painted girders supporting the span. The path here is overhung by hawthorns, and a brimstone butterfly fluttered by. The next bridge, unnumbered, carries the main A45 trunk road but, before that, you pass between the odd brick walls of what was once another little railway bridge that carried the branch line from Blisworth Junction Station to Northampton. Bridge 48 appears, at Gayton Junction, and you must use it to cross to the left bank of the canal to stay on the main line. The right bank will take you on the 4¾-mile-long Northampton Arm. At this point you are told Brentford is 77 miles behind you and Braunston 16½ miles ahead. This is Blisworth Arm or Arm End with its permanent moorings. The towpath is now a rough, grassy walk and you should be careful not to trip over mooring rings.

Next you must use Bridge 47 to take you on to the right bank once again; the bridge is divided into two parts, one for traffic and one originally used to take the horses to the other bank. The canal and the railway keep close together now although, here at least, the only evidence of the line is the noise of the trains. You are now into a surprisingly quiet stretch of the canal which makes for delightfully peaceful walking. You pass under the single girder and iron-rail span of an accommodation bridge, 46. The railway appears on your left while the path narrows a little and becomes a green, clovered way. To your left you can just about see the tips of the square tower of Gayton church, and the canal goes through a fairly shallow cutting with low embankments on either side swathed with the usual canal-side shrubbery. Go under the rather pleasing old stone arch of Bridge 45 where the rubbing bars must have long since disappeared so that the stone itself has been worn away. The accommodation Bridge 44 still has its brick supports but, once again, the span is now wooden – also quite narrow.

Ahead, where the canal bends, it seems as though there is almost a funnel of trees leading you to Bridge 43, Banbury Lane Bridge, built of iron-stained Northamptonshire stone and, by the side of it, there is a white-painted house with its beautifully kept side garden leading directly down to the canal. Beyond there are some old red-brick, canal-side buildings. Here the railway and the canal almost come together, but not quite. In about another half-mile Bridges 41 and 40 come in quick succession. There is

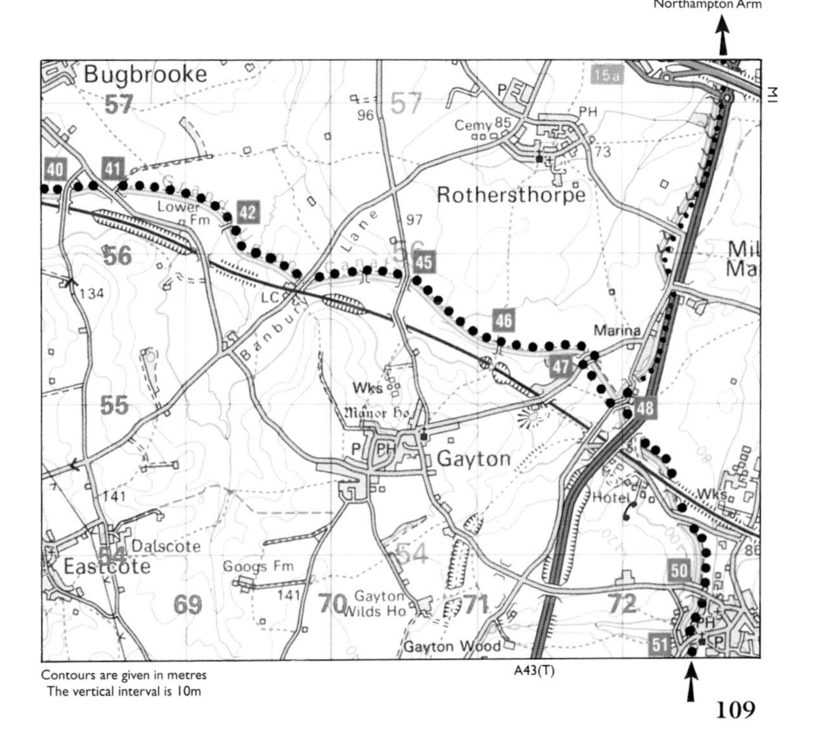

no longer a Bridge 39 and after Bridge 38 comes 36, carrying the B4525 into Bugbrooke and, beside it, the *Old Wharf Inn*. The character of the vegetation to either side changes: at first, with a bit of imagination, you could believe you were chugging along with Humphrey Bogart and Katherine Hepburn aboard the *African Queen* through dense, World War I, African jungle: the canal seems to have metamorphosed into a narrow, sluggish waterway, doomed to divide and eventually disappear. And then the scene changes and you enter what could be a mixed young woodland with the slender trunks of young trees in a state of some disorder.

Hard by Bridge 35 there is a grand red-brick house with a little tree platform in the fork of an old willow by its side. Then, on the far side of the water, some unexpected rocks provided a little island populated by a family of mallard. Round the lefthand bend you come to Bridge 34, an old, cracked and cement-rendered, brick affair. Ahead the canal is quite straight and there is a tall hedge on your right with a pleasant open meadow to the left. On the hill in front, there is a red-brick house with standing sentries of pencil cedars. In the sunshine the fields to the left were lovely, green and rolling but marred just a little by the transmission towers striding across them. Here, because the bank has been quite badly eroded, steel piles have been inserted, linked by rods to anchor piles under the towpath. Powerlines cross the canal with a buzz and a crackle before you approach Bridge 33, another accommodation bridge. The railway is close by on your left again.

You pass by the landing stages of Furnace Wharf at Nether Heyford before you get to Bridge 32 which comes into sight around a righthand bend. There are various boats moored here, mainly pleasure cruisers. There are three or four recently renovated cottages hereabouts and the village is a little way off to your right. The bridge itself looks like an old one, reinforced and repaired comparatively recently, with only the underside of the arch in its original brick. The going underfoot has now improved. The canal then starts to turn sharply to the right and, where it does, a family of ducks was lazing on the far bank. Another skein of powerlines passes, less noisily this time, over the canal where it turns sharply to the left. As you approach some white cottages, on the apex of the bend, listen for the clucking and gobbling of a mixed collection of fowl. For some distance on either side of the cottages, the towpath has been carefully tended so that it is almost lawn-like. The fields opposite are rolling arable, taking your eye to the hilly horizon. By a mile post, the going becomes unkempt again after you pass by a narrows, where brick piers indicate there was once a swing bridge.

All these twists and turns arose because the canal builders were contouring to avoid the expense and time of building locks. The canal takes a turn to the right, with an old willow tree on the inside of the bend and ahead there is a little orchard or plantation hemmed in by a neatly trimmed hedge. You soon come to Bridge 29, now rebuilt in ugly concrete but, by it, there is a tall red-brick dwelling with an ivy-clad end gable and chimney stack. Beyond there are the buildings of Waterways Services. The canal continues to bear to the left, and you soon come to Bridge 28 but, just before you reach it, there is a winding hole. On the left of the bridge there is a collection of farm buildings with Northampton stone gable-ends. Beyond Bridge 28, the sloping canal-side meadow is used as a caravan and camping site which must be a pleasant location for the campers, though a less pleasant sight for canal users. This would be an ideal place for overnighting anglers to make camp. The canal continues to bear round to the left and then turns a little right where there are moorings and a house or two. These are at Bridge 27 where Flore Lane Wharf, now private dwellings, has its neatly trimmed

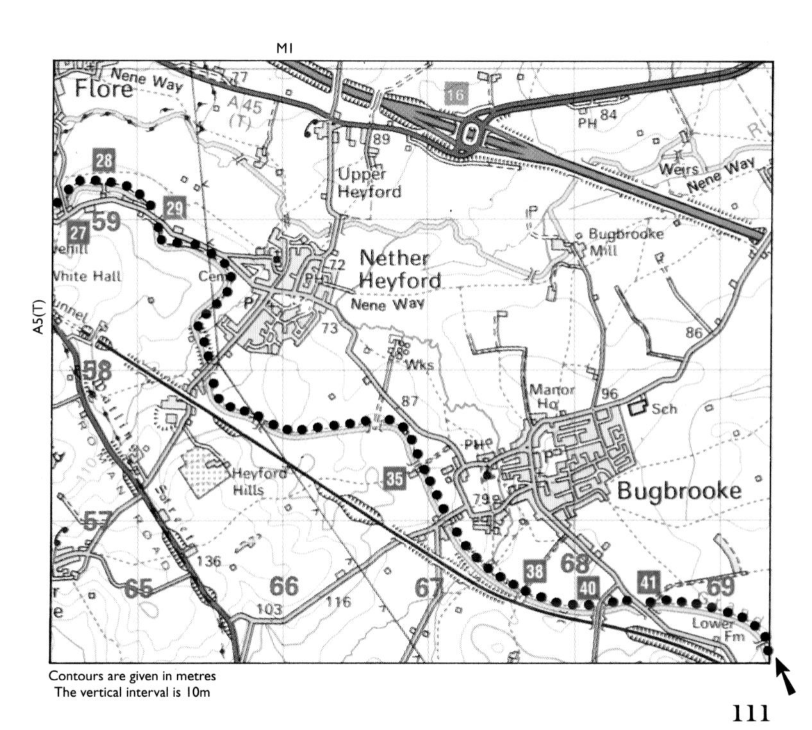

Contours are given in metres
The vertical interval is 10m

lawns edging the canal. Pass by an overflow weir with willowherb growing between its concrete partitions. Here more old industrial buildings have been converted into private dwellings which now back on to the canal where fine willow trees trail their branch tips in the water. Then a large modern bungalow with fine old outbuildings has its back meadow sweeping down to the canal which then bears to the left once more. Canal users are asked to slow because of moored boats, and the towpath becomes narrow and uneven with metal bars and concrete flagstones smoothed by passing feet, set to trip the unwary.

Pass by Stowehill Marine Boat Builders, where there is also *The Narrowboat* public house and motel, with a garden coming down to the canal. This is just before you get to Bridge 26. Where the canal turns to the right, and the railway approaches you fast on the left, you have Bridge 25 and you are on the outskirts of Weedon. Beyond the quite wide red-brick span you soon see, on the opposite bank, the neatly trimmed lawns and

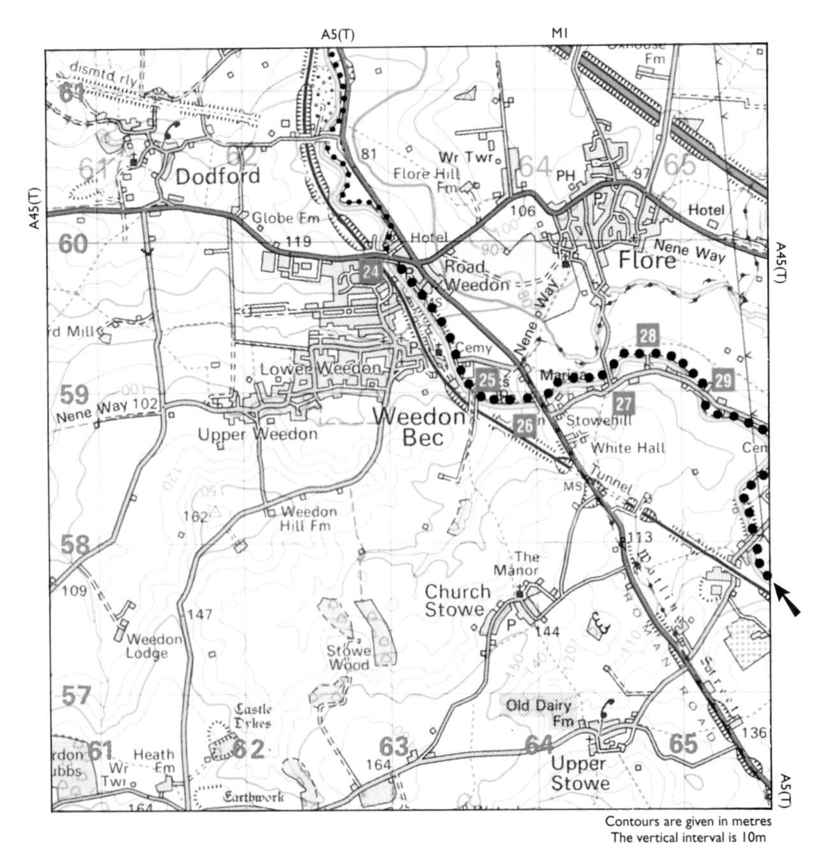

Contours are given in metres
The vertical interval is 10m

A fisherman enjoys the calm of the Northampton Arm at Gayton.

red brick of Weedon Wharf, now a private dwelling. As is often the case when you pass near to any sizeable habitation, the towpath is well used and firm underfoot. You can see the solid-looking Northampton-stone tower of Weedon church rising just above the canal embankment on your left and, as the canal straightens out, Bridge 24 lies ahead. This carries the busy A45. As you pass Concoform Marine, look out for the railway bridge over the former Weedon Military Branch. In the early years of the railway, the stationmaster would have had to remove the rails every time an ammunition boat entered the Ordnance Depot beyond!

The Northampton Arm

5 miles (8 km)

The Northampton Arm begins from Gayton Junction and links the Grand Union Canal with the River Nene in the heart of Northampton. From there it is possible for narrow boat users (provided they are willing to tackle the plethora of locks) to reach the waterways of the Fens and finally the Wash. While the approach to Northampton itself can hardly be said to be scenic, the first 3 or 4 miles of the towpath are certainly worth exploring.

Walk past the canal-side maintenance yard, and the impressive private house beyond with its distinctive chimneys – a trademark of Thomas Millner, the GJCCo. canal engineer from the late 1890s until the 1930s. The first bridge you encounter on this arm is Number 2; it is a turnover bridge and you use it to cross the arm on to the right bank. There is Gayton Marina on your left and many of the boats moored here bear the names of birds such as *Jackdaw, Woodlark, Pied Wagtail, Stonechat, White Stork, Rook.* Although this is a pleasant grassy way, the busy A43 trunk road does follow the arm here and the noise from the traffic can be intrusive. Just before you get to Bridge 3, you pass by a mobile home, its presence sufficiently permanent that it can boast neatly trimmed lawns reaching down to the water. And here, in autumn and winter, there might be the smell of coal-burning in the air from the stoves of moored narrow boats. On the left bank there is a fine line of hawthorn bushes and, through these, you can glimpse the gently rolling Northamptonshire farmland.

You soon come to the first of the 13 Rothersthorpe Locks (**A**) with its lock cottage recently refurbished and hung with tiles on its upper storey. The arm was built 'narrow', with its locks just wide enough for one narrow boat, about 7 feet (2.1 m). Then comes Bridge 4 which leads to Rothersthorpe to the west. Pass beneath it and carry on along the towpath to the next lock. Beyond Lock 3 there is a fine stand of bullrushes – more properly called reedmace. By the tail of Lock 5 is the first of the distinctive lift bridges to be found on the arm. For safety reasons, the bridge is now chained open but it is in good repair. Through this flight of locks, the walking is along pleasantly mown grass which makes for comfortable going. From here, you can now see the town of Northampton itself occupying the high ground ahead and to the left. Notice that the pounds between the locks are very much wider than the locks themselves; this is to provide a head of water to keep the locks filled.

Bridge 6, once another lift bridge, is no longer in place at all; indeed, its remains lie forlornly on the bank before you get to Lock 11. Pass beneath the brick-piered concrete span carrying the link road between the A43 bypass and the M1 and, almost immediately, go beneath the motorway itself, noting perhaps the diffference between bridge architecture on this early motorway and newer structures. The bridge had stood long enough to be decorated with moss and lichens as well as a display of graffiti. Then comes the second link road bridge. Here, as we passed through, a heron seemed indifferent to the roar of motorway traffic and flapped lazily along the canal. Next comes Lock 13 and a lift bridge, Number 8, and for a while the canal runs arrow-straight.

Cross a tributary of the River Nene. Here and there, the canal becomes very narrow but soon you come to Wootton Lock and the brick-built span of Bridge 9 beyond it, its presence foretold by an increase in the number of anglers. (A notice proclaims that the WRCWMC Angling Club controls the fishing rights here and we wondered who could boast such impressive initials.) On the other side of the canal, horses grazed peacefully in the meadows while, further on, they were replaced by cattle on the other side of the canal's low embankment. Before making a gentle turn to the left, the canal goes through another narrows and here the going underfoot would be good in most conditions.

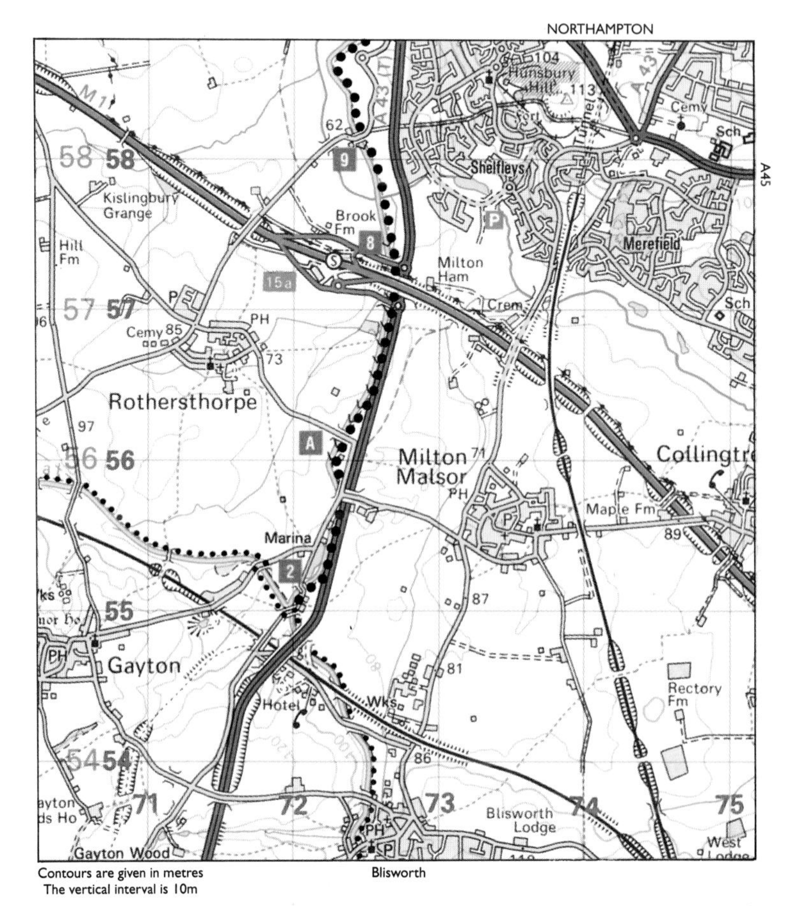

The canal now makes a sharp bend to the east, the right, and, if you look across the water beyond the line of old willows, you can catch a glimpse of Duston Mill **(B)** and, just beyond, the raised banks which obscure the River Nene. In the distance is the Northampton 'lighthouse', a tall concrete tower which dominates the countryside and has nothing to do with ships at sea; instead, it is used by the Express Lift Company to test their products! Go on under the ugly, low, concrete span carrying the A45 at the roundabout where it links with the A43, and you can now see the river on your left with sheep grazing between it and the canal. On your bank ahead, the canal is embellished with a fine stand of *Phragmites* reeds, and this arm, like other parts of the canal, provides a country corridor in an increasingly urbanized landscape. You soon come to Hardingstone Lock, Number 15. Somehow, Bridge 13 seems further away than you expect and, when you reach it, you find that its brick balustrade has now been topped by steel crash barriers. Here, as we passed through, with the towers and office blocks of Northampton in view, a pair of moorhens cackled and splashed busily.

Soon, on your right, just beyond the railway, you can see the chimneys of a housing development. But even though you are close to the heart of a large town, there are still cattle grazing the rough pasture by the canal. At first, the railway to your right is largely concealed by trees but, as you approach Bridge 14, it emerges from the trees and beyond it there is a housing estate with an attendant recreation ground. For some reason, Lock 16 has been partially, though ineffectively one would have thought, defended by a tubular iron railing, and beyond it you pass beneath the railway. You now seem to have entered that no-man's land between good country walking and the heart of the town but, even here, there is a head-bobbing moorhen or two. Suddenly, though, the heavy, pungent smell of organic solvents fills the nostrils, and after some brick moorings, you enter the heart of warehouse land where high barbed-wire-topped, chain-link fencing keeps unwanted visitors to the canal side.

Pass beneath an old brick-piered, steel-girder-spanned bridge and ahead there is the red livery of a Kentucky Fried Chicken fast food establishment and a DIY supercentre alongside. Beyond that is the Carlsberg Northampton Brewery where 'Danish' lager is brewed under licence. Next you come to a low, concrete road bridge. Climb the steps and cross the bridge towards the razzmatazz of the retail park. From the bridge you can see the black warehouse that used to be a thriving source of cargoes for narrow boats, before coming to Lock 17 where the Grand Union links on to the River Nene; it is possible for intrepid walkers to continue on the towpath but it is hardly pleasant. Our preferred route continues at the northern end of the road bridge by picking up the route of the Nene Way to the right. Follow the riverside terraces round, close under the gaze of the Carlsberg complex. When the path reaches the next road, adjoining a three-arched bridge over the river, cross the road with care and continue along the splendid riverside walk until the next lock is reached. Set in a cathedral of trees, this is a fine finish to an interesting arm.

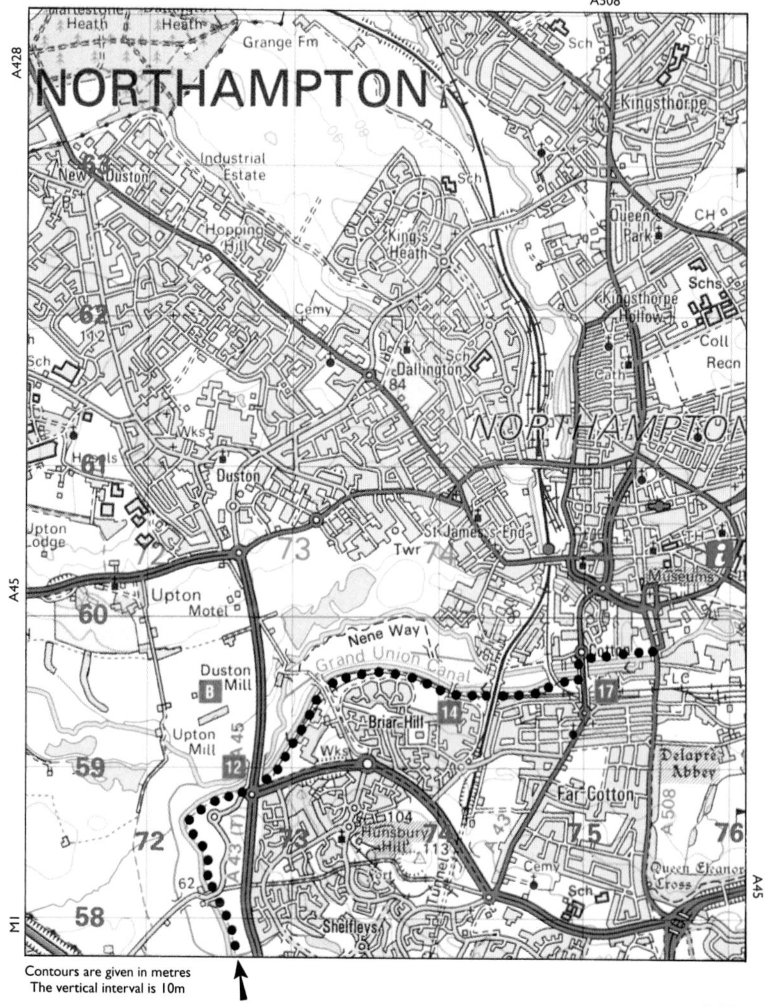

Regimental precision at Weedon barracks beside the now disused arm of the canal.

WEEDON DEPOT

About a third of a mile (500m) north of Weedon Church and about half as far to the west of the Grand Union Canal stand the early nineteenth-century Stores Buildings of the former Royal Ordnance Depot. Surrounded by a high brick wall, the eight original stores are arranged in two lines on each side of a branch of the canal. The cut between the main channel and the depot has now been filled in and built over but the line can still be seen.

The Grand Junction reached Weedon in 1796, the year in which Napoleon defeated Austria. Having already overrun Holland, the French armies were now poised to strike against England, and Napoleon's plans for invasion were no secret.

The English government realized that the storage of military supplies near to the coast was no longer prudent, and plans were made to set up a depot for the storage of arms and ammunition near the centre of the country. A site in Weedon Bec was chosen, possibly because of the proximity of the canal, and, in 1803, an Act of Parliament provided for the acquisition – by what would today be called compulsory purchase – of 53 acres of land from local farmers. The government later extended their estate to about 150 acres.

The canal entered the Depot under a portcullis set in a building known as the East Lodge, part of the surrounding wall. At the west end, there is a similar lodge and the canal originally extended beyond to serve the magazine, used in the early years to store gunpowder, which was delivered by canal boat. The magazine storage buildings, each separated from the other by a building filled with earth, can still be seen from the high ground within the trading estate off the Daventry Road (A45). From here, you can also see a ninth storehouse standing in isolation to the west of the main enclosure. Intended to relieve pressure on the existing army clothing depot at Pimlico, brought about by the South Africa War, it was completed in 1900 just as that war ended.

The trading estate stands upon the site of another of the former military establishments of Weedon, the barracks. Built at about the same time as the Depot, this comprised a group of buildings arranged about a barrack square. Some of these had stables on the ground floor and barrack rooms on the first floor because the barracks was intended to house units of cavalry and infantry. On the platform which can still be made out just inside the fencing south of Cavalry Hill stood the hospital. Between the two world wars, the barracks became the Army School of Equitation, and an extensive indoor riding school and further stables were constructed. The barracks was demolished in about 1960.

The other government buildings in Weedon have given rise to one of the local legends. Constructed in white brick to house the Governor and principal officers of the Depot, the Pavilions, as they came to be known, were well-proportioned buildings with connecting garden walls, presenting an imposing frontage to the east. Two of the buildings were split into two dwellings so that provision was made for five officials in all; these were civilian posts carrying honorary military rank.

At some time, it became popularly believed that the Pavilions were intended to house the King in the event of Napoleonic invasion. Firm evidence for this story is difficult to trace.

The Pavilions were later used as the Officers' Mess of the Riding School, and, during the Second World War, together with the barracks, formed part of the Ordnance Depot, when all parts of the military estate, as well as a number of other buildings in surrounding parts of the country, were dedicated to the provision of weapons to the army in all the theatres of war.

The Pavilions were demolished and replaced by houses in the 1960s, and the Depot was finally closed as an Ordnance Depot on 16 February 1965. Following a period of use by the Ministry of Supply, it passed into private hands in the 1980s and is currently occupied by a number of small companies for stores and workshops.

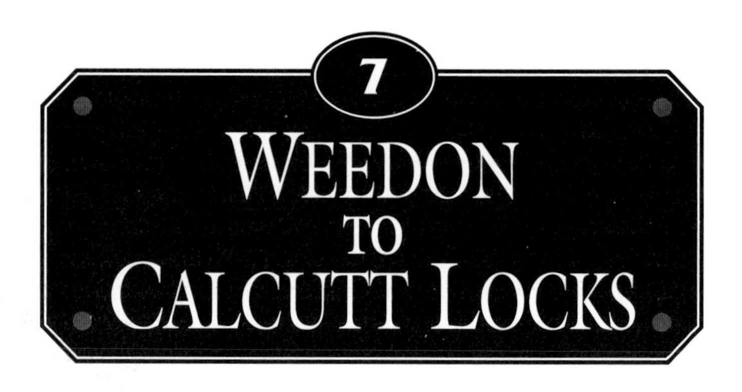

7 Weedon to Calcutt Locks

15 MILES (24.1 KM)

Bridge 24 carries the A45 – one of the main roads that also served the Weedon Depot (see page 118) **(A)**. You can still see the old skew brick arch with a cobbled towpath underneath, but it was extended in 1914 by a girder bridge. The canal now comes very close to the other main road, the A5, following the route of Roman Watling Street. The towpath is screened from the traffic by a blackthorn hedge; it was originally layered but the new shoots have been allowed to grow vertically. This section of the route runs through a very undulating landscape, and the canal follows the contours of the land, swinging through a series of curves that give it a very natural appearance. The canal's wavering path contrasts with the line of the railway which, over the next few miles, alternates deep cuttings with high embankments. This is a very attractive part of the walk with a spattering of farms, perched up on little hillocks or snuggling down into hollows, and surrounded by fields of grain and pasture. Up ahead there is a glimpse of a rather grand manor, Brockhall Park **(B)**, set among formal parkland studded with trees.

Bridge 23 is a particularly good example of a skew bridge, beyond which is a very pleasant rural section, where trees of great variety hang down over the waterway, which include among their numbers the Turkey oak, with a trunk that appears to have been borrowed from a conifer. Beyond Bridge 21 there is a startling contrast. The canal runs towards the parkland of Brockhall. With its carefully arranged trees in a broad park, this is typical of the landscaped grounds that followed and imitated the patterns set in the eighteenth century by the great gardeners such as Capability Brown. However, the remorseless intrusion of the twentieth century is unavoidable as the M1 approaches ever closer to the waterway. Bridge 19 is one of the most impressive along the reach, as befits its role of carrying the driveway up to the hall. The familiar red brick is enlivened by the use of blue engineering brick to define the arch and for the string course, while the parapet is topped with stone. There is a tremendous contrast between the quiet waters of the tree-shaded canal and the trucks roaring past just a few yards away. Here three generations of transport come close together: the eighteenth-century canal is in the middle, with the nineteenth-century railway to one side and the twentieth-century motorway to the other. This is another place

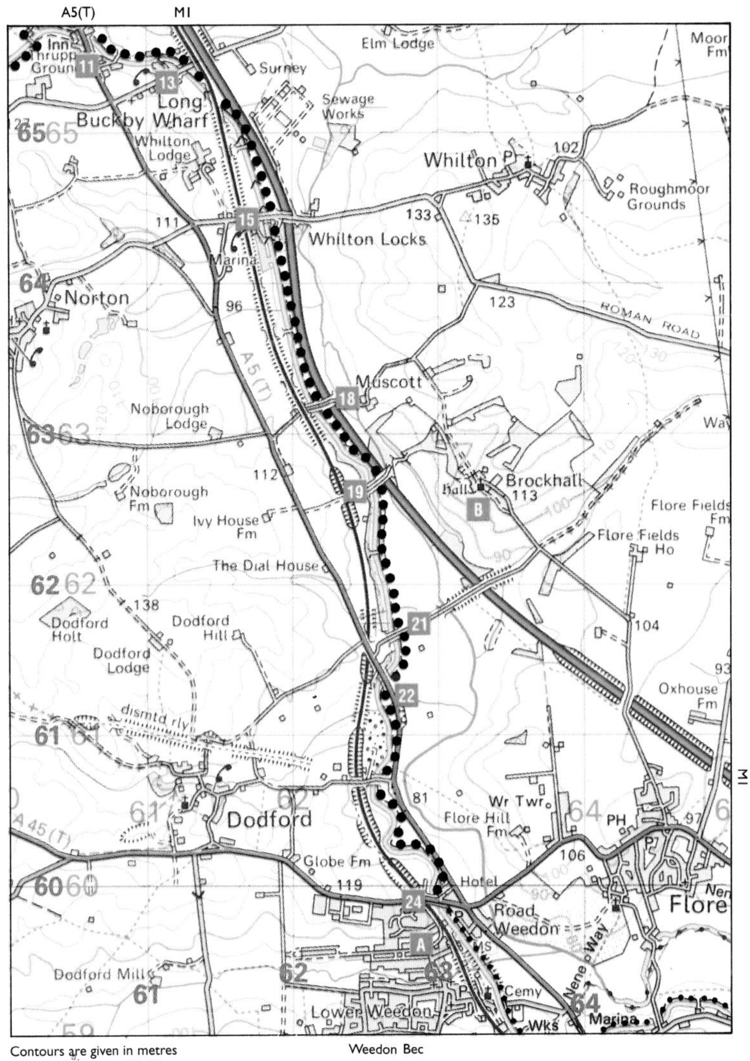

where the differences between railway and canal engineering are made plain. The railway can dive into the hillside in a cutting, but the canal prepares for a steep climb up the Whilton and Buckby locks, seven in all, lifting the canal through 63 feet (19.2 metres).

The locks show ample signs of activity past and present. Crumbling brickwork at the canal edge shows evidence of an old wharf area, and boats queue for the locks, while a great many more remain stationary and firmly moored in Whilton Marina. You now come to a well-spaced-out stagger of locks with an accompanying spatter of canal-side cottages, clearly dating from the canal age as they turn their faces to the water, with arched alleyways linking the canal to the road. The locks themselves are full of interest with features that include old wooden bollards worn into sculptured forms by decades of use and, at the top of the flight, side ponds, now overgrown with reed, but in summer a popular haunt for dragonflies. As well as the cottages that grew up alongside the canal, there is a handsome house on the opposite bank with Gothic windows and lawns reaching down to the canal, where weeping willow drape their branches over the water.

As you approach Bridge 11 the path dives under the busy A5 in a 'people pipe', a tunnel specially built for this long-distance

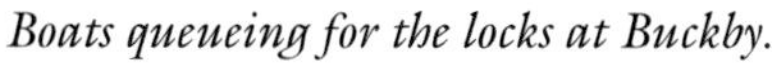
Boats queueing for the locks at Buckby.

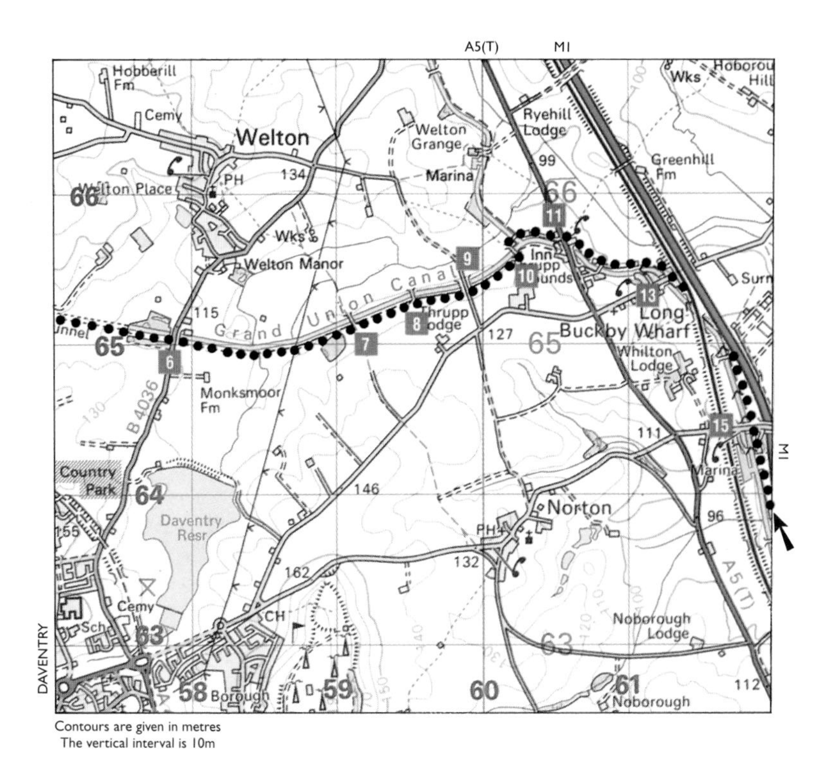

Contours are given in metres
The vertical interval is 10m

walk. At the top lock, cross the canal and continue to follow the towpath on the opposite bank. A house of the local rich goldeny-red ironstone marks the arrival of Norton Junction, where the Leicester Arm of the Grand Union leads away to the right. The old toll office is now a holiday cottage. The towpath now has more of the character of a narrow, riverside walk. Halfway to the next bridge there is a flight of wooden steps. Take these for an easier path along the top of the bank. In places the original concrete edge can be seen, giving an indication of how far erosion has eaten into the bank. The trees have grown up on both sides of the path, so that its old function as a route for horses towing boats has been altogether lost. Over to the left, the tall spire of a church rears up above Daventry, but mostly the canal is in a deep, tree-shaded cutting, a spot much favoured by kingfishers. The canal is now approaching Braunston Tunnel, necessitating a detour. At Bridge 6, go through the arch, then turn left to climb the steps to the path that runs through the woods at the top of the cutting. At the top of the tunnel take the path signposted to Braunston Top Lock. It is a clear path, and the brick tops to the ventilator shafts act as landmarks along the

Peaceful countryside near Norton Junction.

The double elegance of the iron bridges at Braunston.

way. At the main road, cross straight over and continue along the path that runs between hedges to the left of the house. At the far end of the tunnel, take the signposted path at the top of the field, then rejoin the towpath at the top of the flight of six locks that take the canal down, past the old pump house. Braunston is a fine canal settlement that began to grow up when the Oxford Canal first came here. The Oxford Canal itself was improved in the nineteenth century when its course was straightened and the old route was often left as an apparently disconnected arm. Here it is crossed by an iron bridge cast at the Horseley Iron Works. Walking across it, one can see how it is constructed out of standard units with iron plates for the decking and hexagonally patterned railings. The original village of Braunston sits back from the canal on its hill top, dominated by the attractive tower and spire of the parish church **(C)**. Down at water level there is still every evidence of a busy canal world, with boat builders, a dry dock and chandlers. A new marina copes with the modern trade of hire boats, but this is one area where traditional narrow boats are still to be seen, even if they too have been pressed into service for the holiday trade. The Stop House close to the iron bridge now houses an Exhibition

Centre, with changing waterways displays, and gives information on all aspects of the waterways scene. The *Boatman Hotel* has a curious extension with what looks like half a Mississippi steamer stranded on the bank.

At the junction is a particularly splendid pair of iron bridges, forming a double arch. Turn left at the junction and cross the simple turnover bridge, Number 45, that takes the footpath to the other side. This is now part of the Oxford Canal, which was incorporated into the Grand Union system in 1929. Over to the left is the isolated church by Wolfhampcote Hill. The canal is carried on the high bank – Braunston Puddle Banks – built as part of the Oxford Canal improvements, designed to take the extra traffic arriving along the Grand Junction. Bridge 97 is a railway bridge which once serviced a line that has not lasted anything like as well as the canal. The Great Central Railway was the last main line to be built into London; opened in 1899, it was closed in 1963. A second railway crosses and recrosses the canal. This was a branch line from Weedon to Daventry, first suggested in 1845, argued over for forty years and finally opened in 1888: it failed to reach its centenary.

This part of the towpath is in very poor condition, badly overgrown and, in parts, severely eroded. At the time of writing, plans for improvements are in hand but at the moment it can

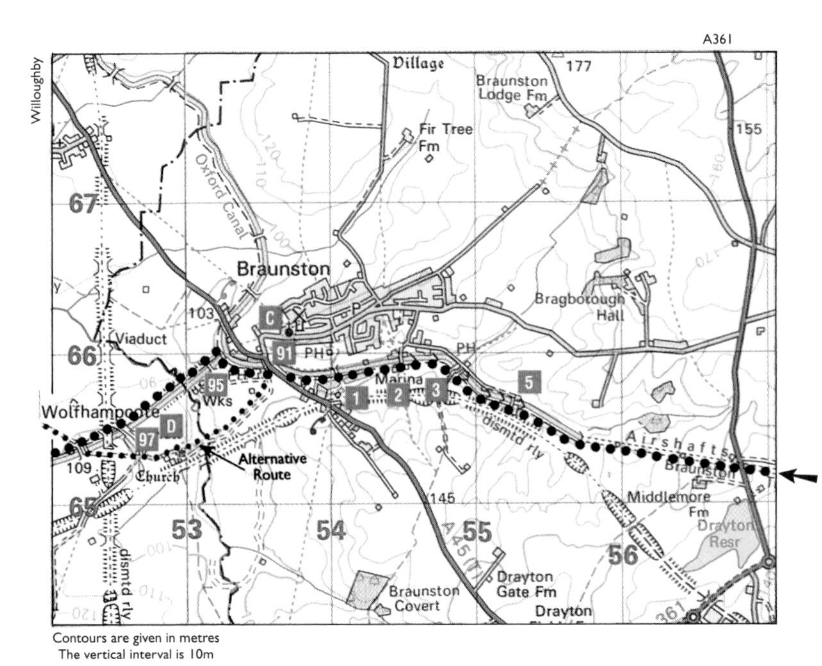

Contours are given in metres
The vertical interval is 10m

only be recommended to those stalwarts determined to do the whole course in spite of scratches from brambles, stings from nettles and the risk of a twisted ankle in a pothole. Those who choose to continue are rewarded by some appealing scenery and they can visit the curious little gothic church of Lower Shuckburgh. Fields by the canal show the 'fossilized' remains of a medieval landscape: the old ridge and furrow of the plough grassed over in Tudor times. The view is dominated by Napton Hill, with its prominent restored windmill. At Napton Junction turn right to continue up the Grand Union past the canal reservoirs, now home to flocks of waterfowl, to Calcutt Locks. This canal was originally the Warwick & Napton, built with narrow locks, and widened as part of a huge improvement scheme after it was incorporated into the Grand Union.

Those who do not fancy the tortuous towpath can reach this point by taking the following diversion from Braunston. Leave the canal at Bridge 91 just before *The Boatman* hotel. At the road, with the bridge behind you turn right on to the path signposted to Wolfhampcote Church. Where the path divides, turn left towards the long embankment of the disused railway.

The route passes isolated Wolfhampcote church, much altered over the years, but with its old square tower still standing. Humps and bumps appear in the field to the right, all that remains of a once thriving village **(D)**. The earthworks nearest

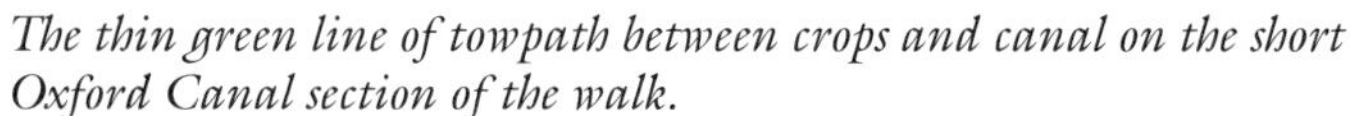

The thin green line of towpath between crops and canal on the short Oxford Canal section of the walk.

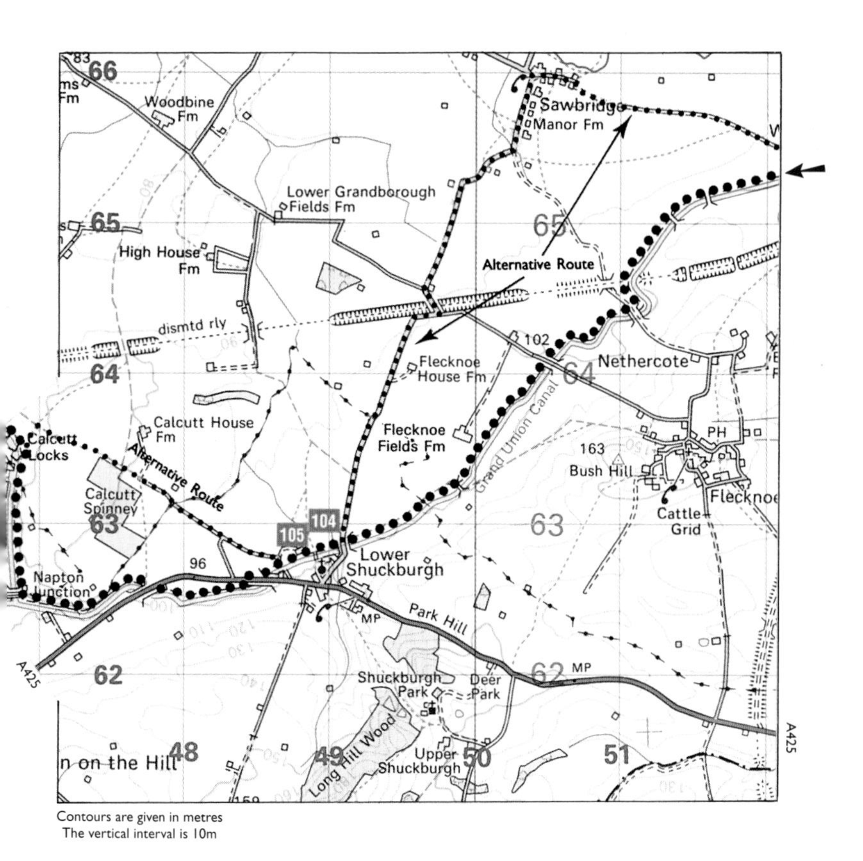

Contours are given in metres
The vertical interval is 10m

the path are those of a hexagonal moat round the old manor and a long fish pond. Continue following the obvious track, crossing the traces of the old Oxford Canal, abandoned when the new junction was created – there was actually a short tunnel at this point, now filled in. Continue straight on over the disused cutting of the Grand Central Railway and over the new line of the canal. The track continues to the hamlet of Sawbridge and passes between the houses. At the road, turn left. At the road junction, turn left to cross the railway bridge, then immediately right, heading for Lower Shuckburgh. Rejoin the towpath at Bridge 104 and turn right, pass Bridge 105 and leave the canal to the right by the remains of the next bridge, now demolished. Turn left on to the obvious track; after a short distance the metalled track turns right. Continue across the field on the footpath that heads off past the small wood. Take the path beside the wood to the gate. At the gate turn left and follow the hedge to the iron gate which leads through to the canal.

8

CALCUTT LOCKS TO KINGSWOOD JUNCTION

20 1/4 MILES (32.6 KM)

The alternative route rejoins the towpath at Calcutt Locks, the start of the descent from the Oxford Canal, and you now continue on, between hedgerows, past a small marina to Bridge 18, a modest footbridge – a curiosity of this canal is that bridge numbering starts with the junction bridge at Number 17. The original plan was for a wholly new canal from Braunston to Warwick and, though the plan was never realized, the numbering remained. Bridge 19 is a much grander, skew bridge but there is little change in the scenery. The path is still bordered by a hawthorn hedge and the canal itself has a reedy margin, popular with yellowhammers. Where there are gaps, the view opens out to agricultural land, fields and hedgerows and a spattering of farms. Taller trees, mainly elder and birch, have grown up in the hedge and there are glimpses of the abandoned railway alongside. Bridge 20 is known as Gibraltar Bridge, suggesting rocks, and there are indeed quarries nearby, with confirmation of some sort of activity in a narrow basin, now overgrown with weeds, that leads off to the left towards a high wooded hill. A road runs along beside the wide, grassy towpath, while on the opposite side is a second basin, serving another small quarry, barely glimpsed among the trees **(A)**. As the woods thin out, so rough grassland appears interspersed with fields of clover.

A neat, red-brick bridge, Number 21, and the *Boat Inn* with its narrow-boat sign is followed by an impressive stand of tall birch and a new marina, surrounded by high banks that are gradually being grassed over. Then, a delightful tree-shaded area leads into the ten close-packed locks of the Stockton flight. Here it is especially easy to see the changes made in 1929–30. The old narrow locks, bereft of gates, now serve as overspill weirs for the new broad locks with their smart array of black and white beams and covered paddle gear and their new lock cottage. The pub halfway up, *The Blue Lias*, is named after the local stone, a mixture of limestone and shale – which, incidentally, is not blue but a pale grey. The sign shows a brontosaurus to commemorate the discovery of a fossilized skeleton in a nearby quarry. The *Two Boats* at Bridge 23 requires no explanation – and has suitably boaty pictures inside. The Kayes Arm, where traditional boats can still be seen, heads off in the direction of the tall chimney of the Rugby Cement Works.

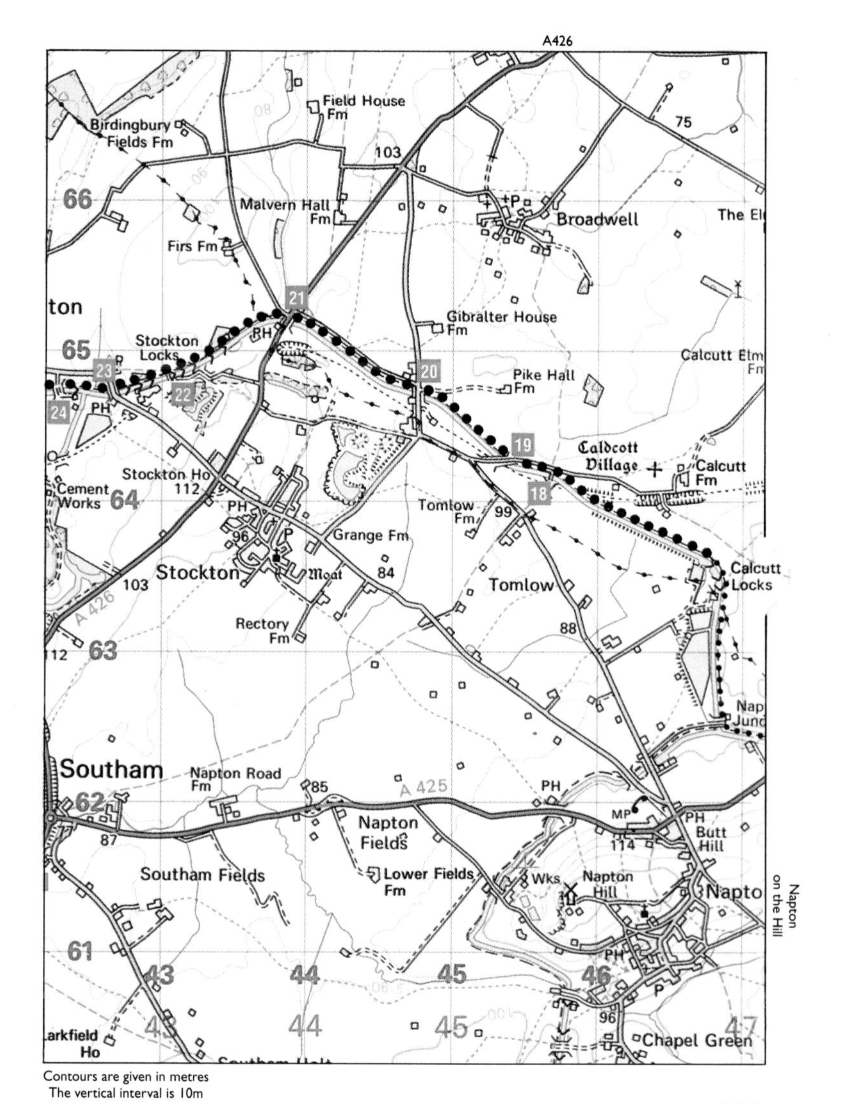

Contours are given in metres
The vertical interval is 10m

Beyond the bottom of the locks, the towpath goes under the concrete Bridge 25 that carries the A423 trunk road, under a conventional canal bridge, Number 26, and over the River Itchen on a short aqueduct. There is a pleasing open aspect of undulating farmland and a view to the right of Long Itchington church tower (**B**). Once again, the old signs of ridge and furrow appear beneath the grassland. The canal perches up on a high bank, but the railway from the cement works comes in at even higher level, striding on a viaduct across river and canal. The path is bordered by a layered hedge, now allowed to grow upwards to a considerable height, but the view to the left remains open. Bridge 27 is a very attractive modern rebuild with stepped ramp, corbelled corner and banded blue and red brick. The canal now swings round the shoulder of a low hill with a grassy bank to the right, speckled with dandelion, willowherb and bindweed in the neatly layered hedge. This is followed by a long straight where trees encroach on the right, but the view to the left opens out on fields of grazing sheep and cattle. There are occasional views of wood-topped hillocks in the distance and, where the land has been ploughed, the soil appears as a lovely deep, rich red.

This section ends at the Bascote Locks, with toll house and lobby at the top. The first two locks are arranged as a 'staircase', running straight into each other, with no intervening pound. The

A pub with a geological message, The Blue Lias near Stockton.

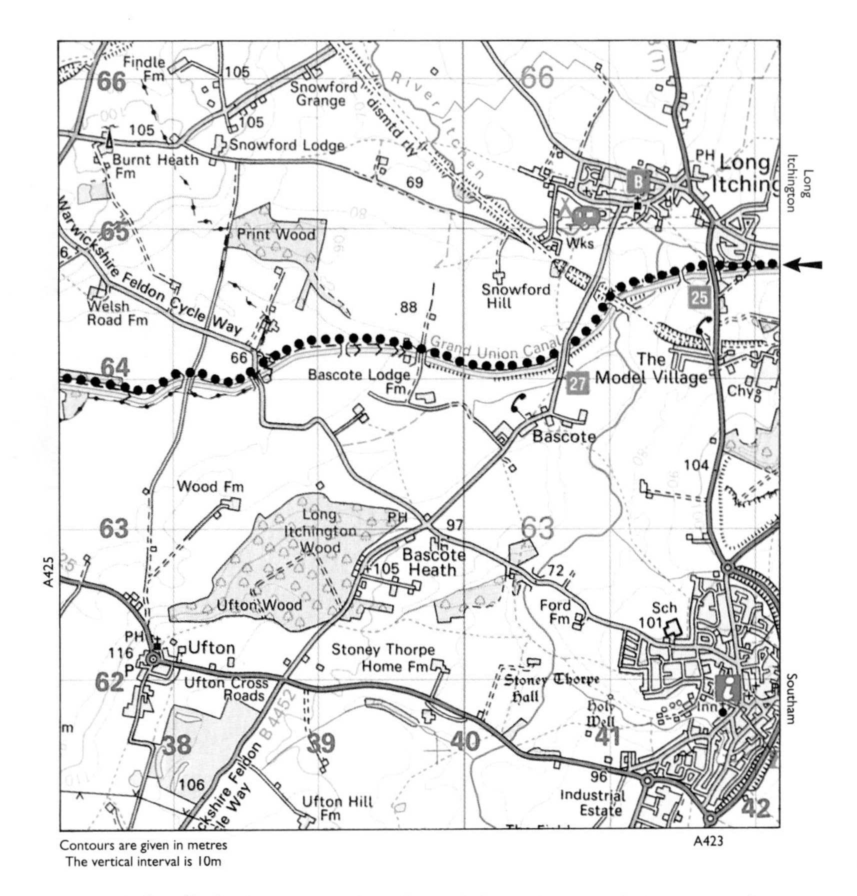

Contours are given in metres
The vertical interval is 10m

rest of the flight is conventional, with broad pounds between the locks, which act as small reservoirs. At the end of the locks the view opens out again to a landscape of small fields bounded by hedgerows, with the occasional tall oak rearing up, and patches of woodland. The canal itself has a margin of reeds and bulrushes. Lock 18 shows the old and the new: the former narrow lock has an 1891 date, but the lock cottage dates from the 1929 widening. Bridge 30 below the lock carries Welsh Road, one of the old drove roads used to bring cattle from Wales to England, but based on a much older route thought to have been made in the Iron Age, the Jurassic Way. The canal continues to wriggle round the natural rises and falls of the landscape. White bryony clambers through the hedgerow and the towpath broadens to a wide grassy track, with stumps of old telegraph poles for accompaniment. Lock 19 appears in isolation with a neatly vaulted brick storehouse alongside. The outlook remains much the same, with the addition of the occasional goat among the grazing sheep and cattle. The fields rise up to a grassy knoll and reeds encroach far into the channel on the approach to Lock 20. Bridge 32 beyond the lock carries another ancient route, the Foss Way **(C)**, the Roman road that extended from Lincoln to Axminster in Devon and marked the boundary of the first Roman province. The local spelling for the locks, surrounding farms and so on is 'Fosse'. There is an attractive old house and wharf by the bridge, with warehouses opening to both road and canal. The three Fosse Locks are spread out over a considerable distance, passing through what is still a very rural landscape where the only buildings in sight are the occasional farms and barns.

Bridge 33 is a lovely affair of gentle curves that scarcely disturbs the horizon, with a background of trees from a narrow strip of woodland that borders the canal. Oaks hang branches over the path and tall beech and horse chestnut rear up in the copse. Radford Bottom Lock appears, framed in an arch of the great skew viaduct that once carried the old LNWR, Leamington to Rugby line. The parkland of Offchurch Manor reaches down to the lock-side, with sycamore and oak providing a dense green background to the lock. The park entrance is marked by a neat verandahed lodge, with mullioned windows topped by drip mouldings. The woods continue to follow the towpath, with poplar striking the dominant note. Glimpses of water flashing in the light beyond the trees show where the River Leam is running alongside. The canal has been carved out of the hillside above the river, and occasionally the rough marl rock can be seen breaking through. The canal curves round to follow the river valley, an attractive section with a reedy winding hole overshadowed by willow. At the approach to Radford Semele more exotic species, rhododendron and pine, appear among the trees and a long overspill weir carries excess water away down to the Leam. Soon the whole landscape begins to change. The tower of Radford Semele church **(D)** comes into view on the left, while to the right, beyond a rather scrubby wasteland, the tower blocks of Leamington rise up.

Urbanization begins at Bridge 35, marked first by the pyramidal roofs of the former Thornley Brewery, now surrounded by modern industrial units. A small brick aqueduct carries the canal across a brook, then houses appear on both sides. The newer houses to the left have been laid out with grassy areas and canal-side walks; the older houses to the right have gardens running up to the towpath hedge, which is enlivened by the overspill of garden flowers. By *The Fusilier* pub at Bridge 37 there is a mooring area with unusually ornate bollards on fluted columns. The path goes through the old industrial area of Leamington, built up around the canal. There are close-packed terraces and a very Gothic Victorian school, and beyond Bridge 38 factories occupy what was once the site of one of Leamington's foremost industries, the Eagle Foundry. The only hint of fashionable Leamington, the

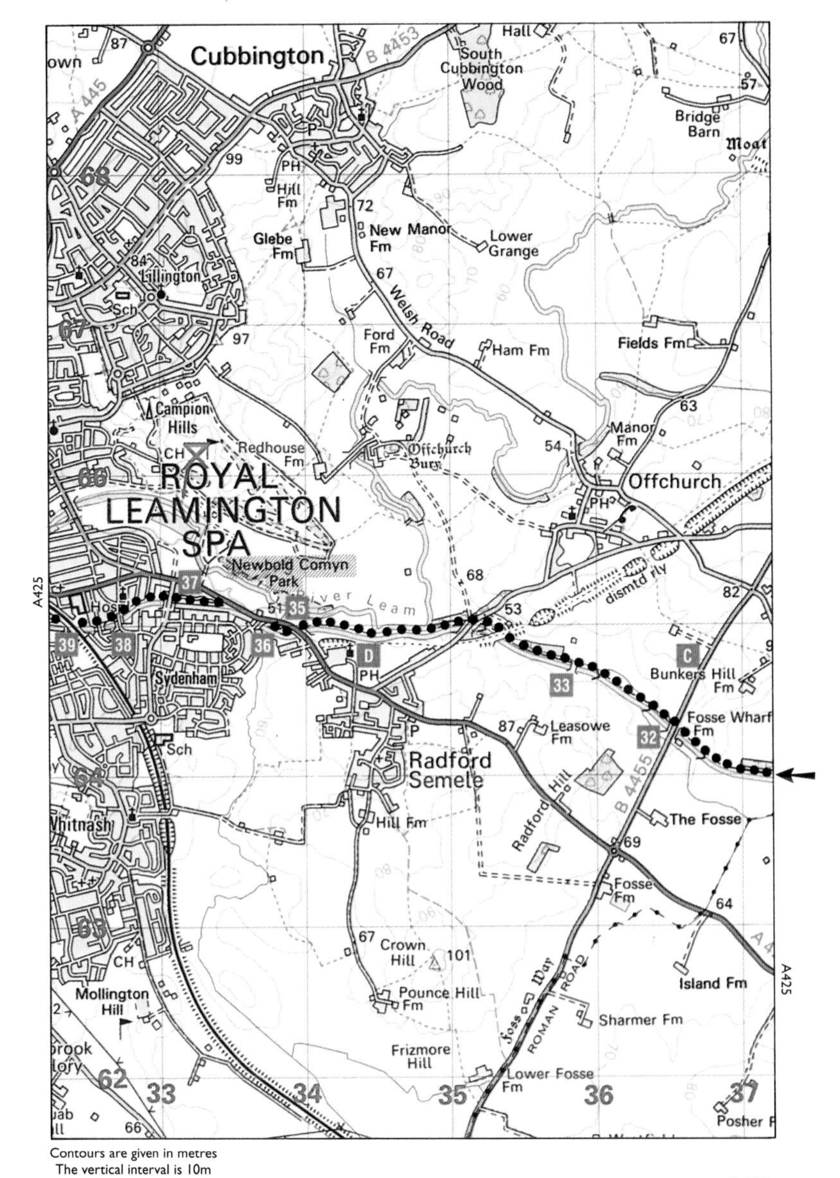

Contours are given in metres
The vertical interval is 10m

spa town, comes at Bridge 40 with a very ornate house and the Grand Union Hotel and Restaurant. Then, at Bridge 41, the town is partly lost from view as the canal dives down through a leafy cutting: it is not, however, out of earshot, for the A425 runs alongside. The canal eventually emerges from the cutting by Ford's Foundry. The sense of being in a very urban environment returns with a paved towpath, and glimpses of a new retail park. An area of new housing seems to have adopted canal themes in the architecture, with two-storey-high bays, reminiscent of loading bays. There is a leafy canal-side walk for the new residents, and the towpath is screened from the main road as Leamington is left behind.

The main railway line from Leamington to Warwick is crossed on a three-arched brick aqueduct in a setting of green fields and, to emphasize the rural interlude, the house by Bridge 45 comes complete with duck pond. The canal now strides across the River Avon on another three-arched aqueduct. There is a distant glimpse of the towers of Warwick Castle, but the canal gets no closer to historic Warwick than it did to the elegance of Leamington. It is possible, however, to leave the canal by steps alongside the aqueduct for a riverside walk to the town centre. The towpath walk meanwhile continues along a high bank, with views out over suburban rooftops. A cluster of bridges follows and beyond the big skew Bridge 48 there is an old area of industrial buildings. Emscote Mills **(E)** is a typical narrow late eighteenth-century factory with segmented arched windows – used for many years for manufacturing gelatine, but almost certainly begun as a textile mill. There are, as one would expect, extensive wharves here, now home to a boatyard that extends up as far as Bridge 49. Although the scenery may not be quite what one expects of Warwick, the canal manages to keep itself to itself, screened from the rest of the world by ash and sycamore and, when houses appear, by ornamental garden plantings ranging from weeping willows to huge clumps of pampas grass.

Having reached the Avon valley, the canal now has to climb again, up towards the Birmingham plateau, starting with the two Cape Locks, with the *Cape of Good Hope* pub at the top. The factories are left behind as the canal heads into a leafy cutting which ends at a group of tall pine trees that marks the entrance to Warwick cemetery. Bridge 51 has been recently rebuilt in traditional form, and beyond it is the Saltisford Arm. This is, in fact, the original route of the Warwick and Birmingham Canal, which ended at Saltisford Basin, so that the walk now leaves the old

A46(T) COVENTRY
10 km or 6 miles

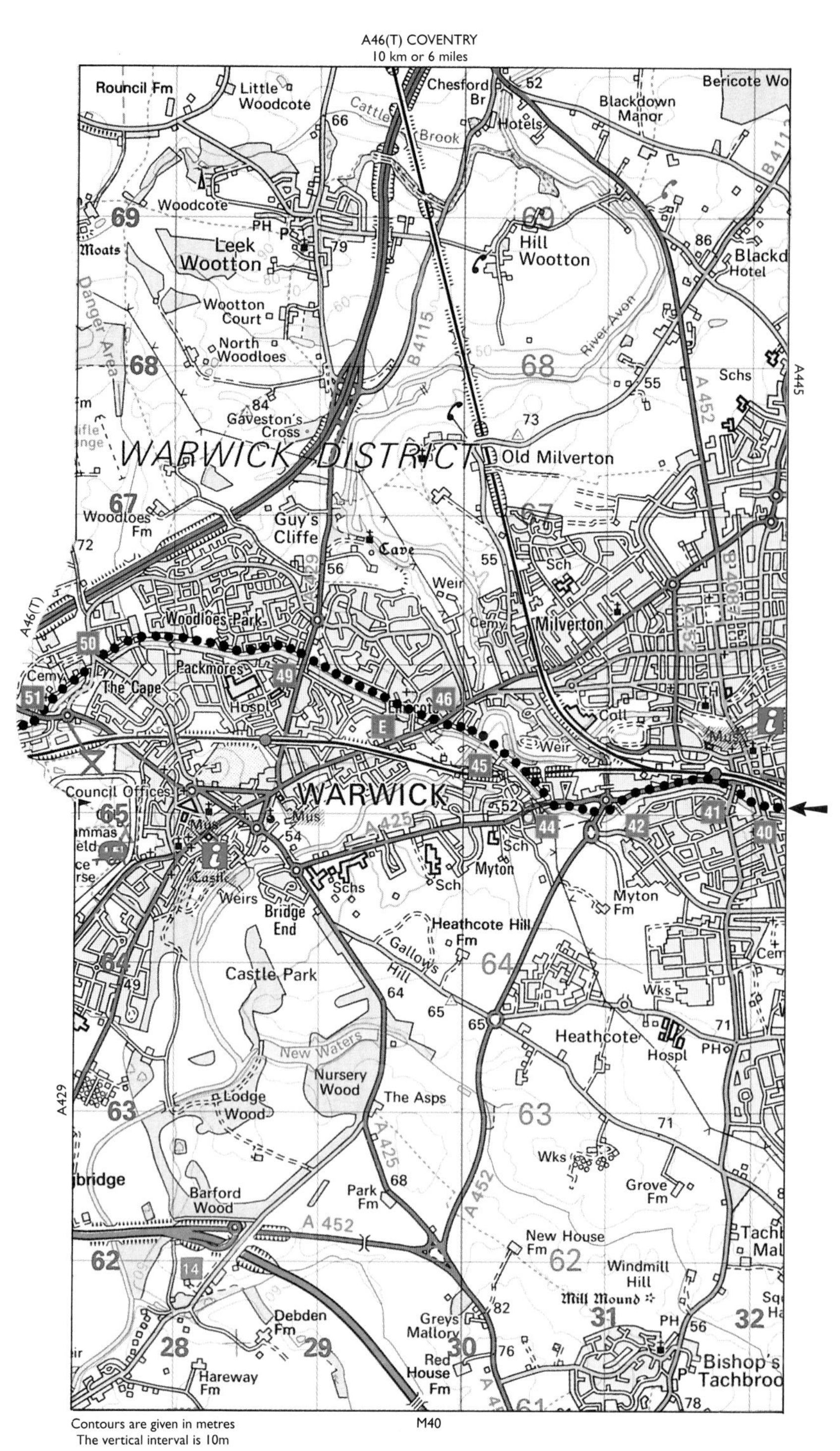

A445

A429

Contours are given in metres
The vertical interval is 10m

M40

Warwick and Napton Canal – but this time, there is no re-numbering of bridges. The canal passes under the modern A46 road bridge to arrive at a lock cottage and the foot of the Hatton Locks.

At first there is no indication that this is anything more than another lock and cottage, but, in fact, there are 21 locks in all, making this one of the most impressive flights in Britain. The walk up the side is particularly pleasant, with a wide grassy tow-path and extensive views. The black and white balance beams stand out smartly against the background of trees and you can see how this canal, too, began with single locks. Past Bridge 52, called, rather unfairly, 'Ugly Bridge', more of the locks start to come into view and, once past the bridge where flowers bloom out of the old masonry chamber, a whole string of locks appears marching off to the horizon. There are canal-side stables by Lock 33 and the houses further up have colourful girders where flowers spill out on to the towpath margins. Bridge 53 brings Middle Lock, a lock cottage and a grand floral flourish. Beyond it is the former Hatton mental hospital and, reminiscent of the Hanwell flight, Asylum Wharf.

Now one is rewarded by one of the most dramatic sights on the canal system as the rest of the locks bunch together to climb straight and steeply up the hill. To ensure there was enough water to operate the locks, extensive side ponds were terraced into the hill between each lock and these, with their reedy margins and waterfall-like weirs, make a happy home for wagtails and yellowhammers. The sombre, dark-blue brick of Hatton maintenance yard, the whitewashed canal offices and the *Waterman Arms* announce that the end of the flight is near. Cross the canal here, at Bridge 54. There is a picnic area and a canal shop with refreshments at the very top. The locks have lifted the canal a total of 146 feet 6 ins (44.5 metres).

An attractive rural section now begins, and the canal is lined by mature oak and sycamore. By Bridge 55 a houseboat has its own garden on the bank, and there is a view over a landscape of fields, hedges and solitary oak trees, while the towpath is bordered by a dense hedge crammed with brambles, beyond which the railway line runs along to Hatton station, close by Bridge 56, where the Mid Warwickshire Yacht Club can also be found. The only thing to mar the peace is the rumble of traffic on the nearby M40 motorway. The view is, however, unspoiled. Charollais and Herefords munch in the fields, and more medieval ridge and furrow can be seen. The canal now dives into the hillside, in a deep,

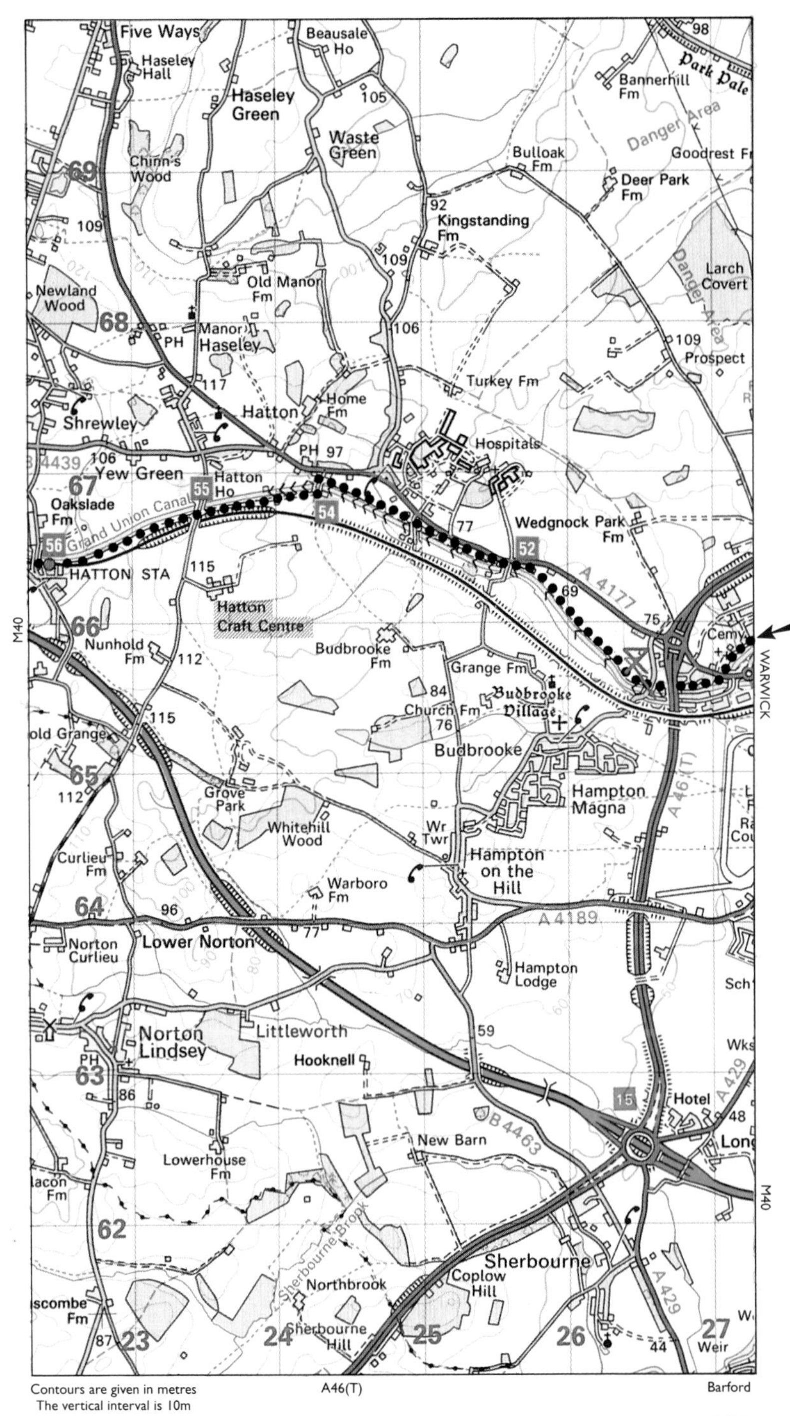

Contours are given in metres
The vertical interval is 10m

A46(T)

Barford

The footpath emerges from the 'horse tunnel' at Shrewley.

tree-hung cutting that leads up to the mouth of Shrewley Tunnel. There is no towpath – boatmen used to pull themselves along by the rails set in the tunnel side. Take the path up by the stone wall to the top of the tunnel and continue, between hedges, to the road. Cross the road and take the path opposite, beside Orchard Cottage. This heads steeply downhill to the horse tunnel, with ridges in the pathway to help the horse keep its footing. It emerges near the top of the tunnel – which drips noisily – and continues on down to conventional towpath level. The deep cutting shows exposed rock strata, marl and sandstone, and is overhung by trees.

The view opens out again – and motorway noise increases – by Bridge 60. The newly ploughed fields have an almost purple richness, and the most prominent house is aptly named 'High Chimneys'. The canal swings round to the right to an area of 'cut and fill' where spoil from the cutting has been used to build up the neighbouring embankment. The bank arrives first, giving walkers a tree-top height stroll and superb views out over fields and houses, before sinking into the cutting, which can be a decidedly damp and muddy place. Then, to avoid more extensive earthworks, the canal hugs the hillside, twisting and turning to follow the contours, until it reaches the peaceful hamlet of Turner's Green, and the *Tom o' the Wood* pub, named after a now vanished windmill. A few more wiggles bring you to a curiously angular Bridge 64, and a hedgerow that sprouts crab apple trees and a large cedar. Then the canal reaches Kingswood Junction: to the left, a short arm leads off to the Stratford Canal while the main walk continues across the bridge and up the long straight.

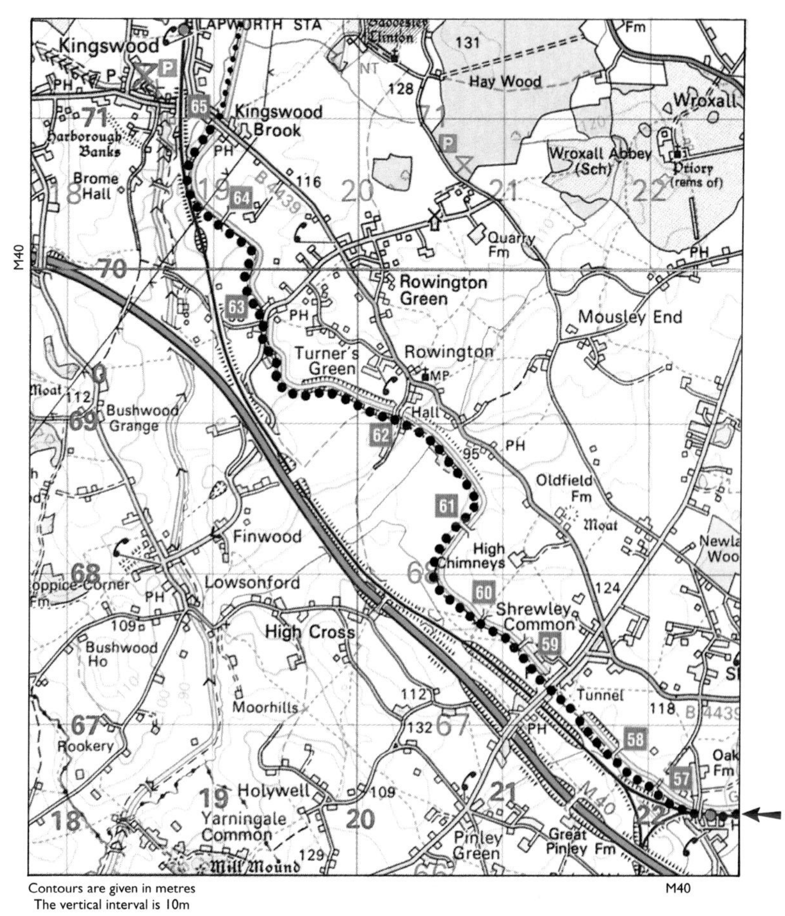

Contours are given in metres
The vertical interval is 10m

M40

Mellow brick and beehive alcoves at Packwood House.

A Circular Walk from Kingswood Junction

4½ miles (7 kms)

At the junction, turn left off the Grand Union towpath, in the direction shown by the signpost for the Stratford Canal. Pass under the railway bridge and beyond the first lock cross over the split bridge, over the end of the Stratford Canal lock by the maintenance yard. Turn right to follow the towpath alongside the Lapworth flight of locks. Continue past the lock cottage and split bridge, which allowed the tow rope to pass through as the horse crossed over, to the top lock, No. 6, and at the next bridge, No. 31, go through the arch and turn left to join the road. At the road, turn left, then immediately right on to the road signposted to Packwood House. Continue straight on at the next road junction up the tree-shaded lane. At the next road junction turn left onto the road past Packwood House. There is a good view of the Tudor house, with its magnificent topiary garden. The road runs between two outbuildings, each with a sundial; one for the morning sun and the other for the afternoon.

At the next road junction, opposite the sign 'Grove Lane', turn right over the stile to follow the footpath in the direction indicated by the yellow arrow. Head across the field for a stile to the right of the line of trees. Cross the stream on the little single girder, and head for the patch of woodland. Follow the side of the wood, then cross the stile to go through the narrow neck of woodland. Continue on down the long avenue of trees. At the road turn right. At the crossroads turn left and continue on this road across the railway and straight on to the canal. At the canal turn right onto the towpath to return to the start.

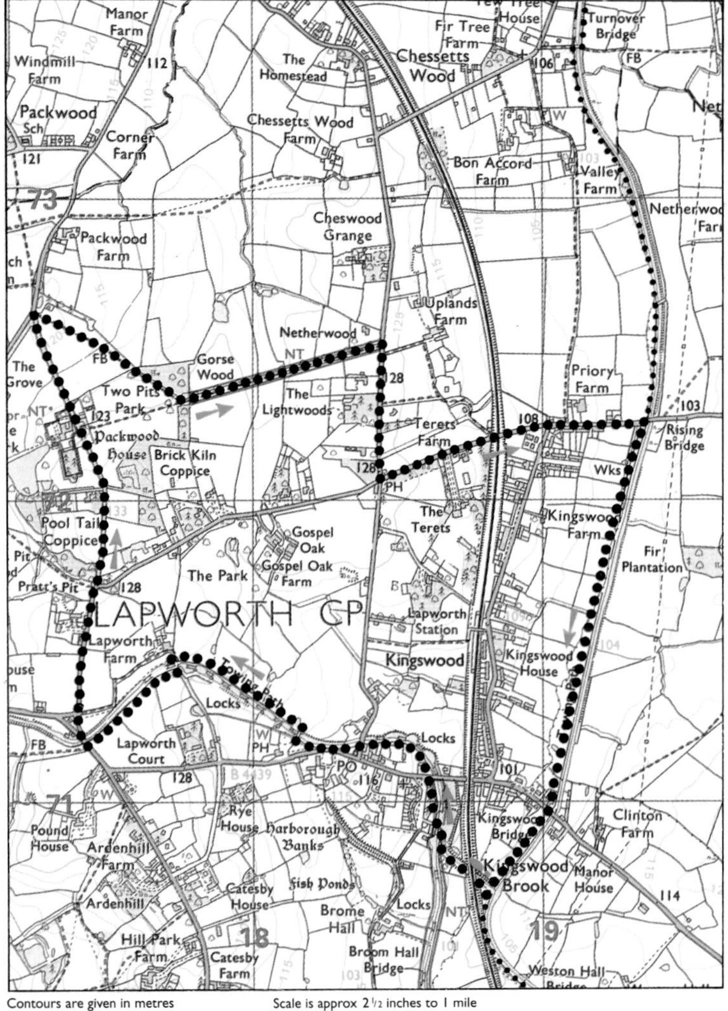

Contours are given in metres
The vertical interval is 5m

Scale is approx 2½ inches to 1 mile

9
KINGSWOOD JUNCTION TO GAS STREET BASIN

17 1/4 MILES (27.7 KM)

The *Navigation Inn* stands by Bridge 65, after which comes a typical section of hedgerow-bordered canal with an accompanying parade of pylons. Bridge 66 marks the boundary between the Trent and the Severn river authorities. The main appeal of this stretch is the wildlife – squirrels abound in the thickets, birds of all kinds can be seen and heard, from a variety of warblers calling from the hedges to pheasant strutting among the fields. Trees close in at places, with willow overhanging the towpath, and there are houses again at Bridge 67, where the towpath again changes side. The path is now broad and grassy, passing through a shallow cutting, dominated by a majestic oak. A small group of buildings appears by the old Bakers Lane Wharf, including a timber-framed farmhouse with an orchard alongside. The canal swings gently round to Bridge 69, where there is some semantic disagreement between the *Black Boy Inn* and the Black Buoy Cruising Club. On either side of the canal are humps and hollows suggestive of a deserted medieval village site – common enough in this area. The canal crosses a small stream, and there is a more open aspect, with a panoramic view of wooded hills, with Knowle Hall half hidden among the trees **(A)**.

Knowle Locks are particularly colourful with flower beds and the name picked out in stone on the grass. The path goes up by the side of the old narrow locks and, curiously, there are six of these replaced by only five new, broad locks. A sign announces that there are now thirteen miles to go to Gas Street, and the end of the walk. At the top of the locks is a canopied wharf building, followed by a tunnel-like road bridge, Number 71, and a cutting overhung by sycamore. As the cutting opens out again, there is a scattering of houses and a solitary but magnificent chestnut tree. Woodland appears at Bridge 72 and echoes to the chattering of magpies and the raucous calls from a rookery. The curved cutting has a somewhat crumbled towpath – there is now a large watery gap between the concrete piling and the path. Bridge 73 crosses the cutting at a high level and ferns grow in profusion along the high cutting sides. Inevitably, the

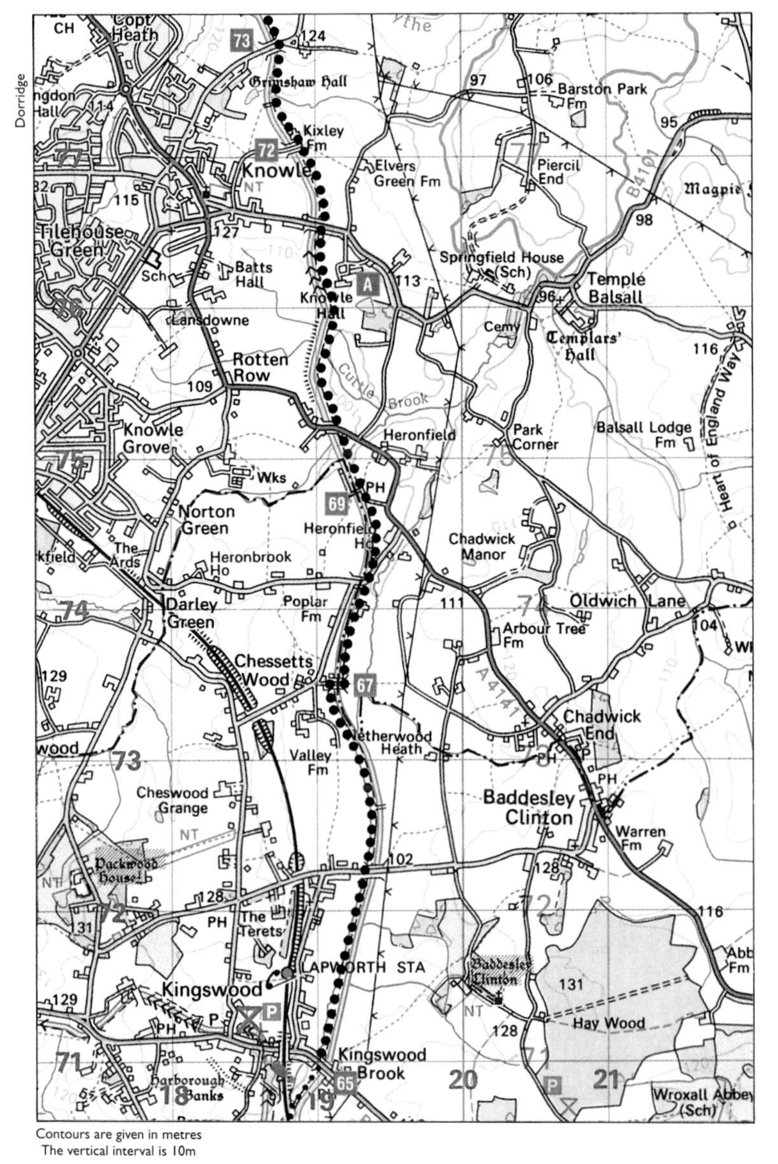

Contours are given in metres
The vertical interval is 10m

cutting is followed by a bank that carries the canal over a tributary of the River Blythe. A pond by Bridge 75 provides a rural note, but the increased noise of traffic, now in view, heralds the arrival of the motorway, and the M42 crosses a little way up ahead, with the old Bridge 76 incongruously tucked away underneath it. Copt Heath Wharf now provides a somewhat noisy mooring, but still looks pleasing with its canal cottage of plain red brick and slate. There is a glint of water below the bank, from the River Blythe, soon to be crossed on a small aqueduct. An overspill weir carries water down from the bank, through the trees to the river. A sharp corner would have caused problems in horse-boat days, with the tow rope catching in the trees, so a stout iron post was set up and now bears the scars of the multitude of ropes that have cut into it.

At Bridge 78 the canal reaches the fringes of the housing developments spreading outwards from Birmingham, in the form of a finger of development pointing out from Solihull. But it is all soon lost from view as the path leads through a steadily deepening cutting, the sides a tangle of bracken ana bramble. Oak trees put out branches over the path so low that the walker often has to duck to get under them. The noise of motorways has gone, but now it is replaced by the sound of jets from nearby

The end is nigh! Signpost at Knowle.

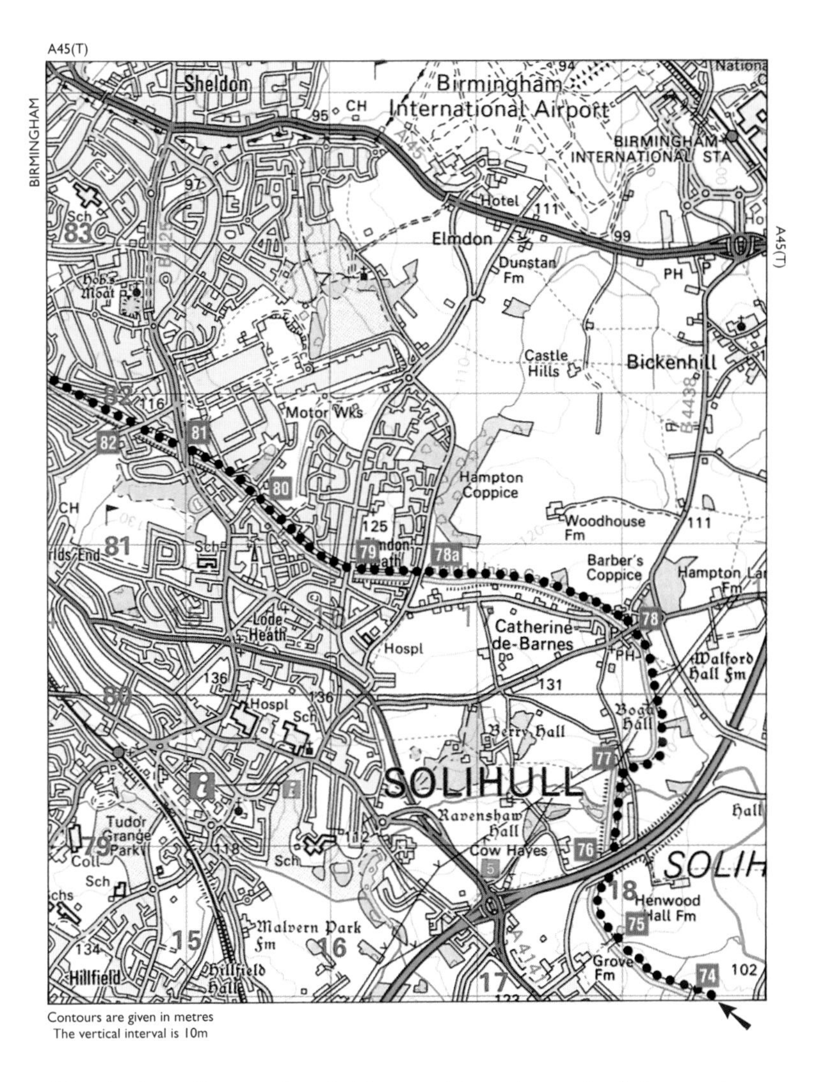

Contours are given in metres
The vertical interval is 10m

Birmingham International Airport. Near the end of the cutting, the canal opens out to the huge British Gas research and administrative centre, which makes a polite nod towards the canal with a tiny garden, but provides no access to the towpath. The opening out of the cutting provides a glimpse, but no more, of houses and light industry. The canal remains enclosed in greenery, and bird song rings out from the bushes and trees – the loud *tink* of a chaffinch and the slightly mournful song of the robin. Oak, birch and sycamore grow up from a mass of fern and bramble. Beyond Bridge 82, where a new concrete bridge has joined the old, tall beech trees dominate. This cutting can be very muddy in wet

Horse ramps provide patterns and texture at Ashtead locks.

weather. By the next bridge, Number 83, cutting has given way to bank and there is a view out over suburban houses, and the illusion of being on a country walk temporarily ends. At Bridge 84 the big Lucas works and industrial estates line the route and the railway comes in on the left, but the margins remain green, dotted with cow parsley and willowherb. Where the view opens it presents a seemingly endless prospect of rooftops. Then, rather surprisingly, at the next bridge, the trees return to enclose the route and only the rubbish high on the bank shows that this is an urban area. Beyond the high arch of Bridge 86 the canal swings round to the left past allotments and a very crowded commercial vehicle yard. There is an extraordinary alternation of moods here. Between Bridges 86 and 86a is a green tunnel, which at Bridge 87 becomes an open area with a view dominated by the towers of Birmingham. A new, metric, distance post announces that there are 8 kilometres to go to Gas Street.

Industry now takes over with a vengeance. A tall spike-topped wall accompanies the towpath, while, opposite, older factories still have canopied wharves. A tall slender chimney stands by the Birmingham City Council Incinerator **(B)**, where a high arched bridge takes the towpath over an arm, long since filled in. There follows an area of factories and scrubby wasteland surrounding the River Cole; this is crossed on an aqueduct which is little more than an arched opening in the bank. In the little basin on the right, the Acker's Trust has its fleet of youth and community boats. Past the railway bridge there is a touch of green with playing fields across the canal, and Bridge 89 displays a feature that is commonplace in the Birmingham area: a little red door in the parapet can be opened to allow firemen to draw up water. The urban scene around Bridge 90 is enlivened by an ornate clock tower and a church spire: across the canal, older factories have walls dropping sheer to the water, while brambles and daisies mass along the towpath.

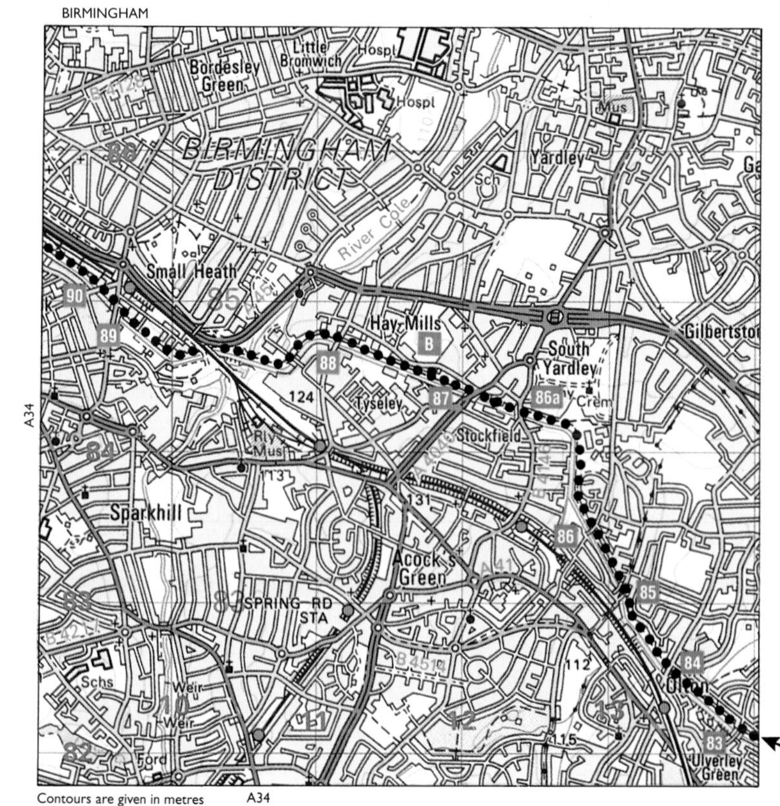

Bridge 91 is a girder bridge, and after that the canal opens out to Camp Hill Basin, surrounded by canopied warehouses. Camp Hill Locks take the canal downhill, but now the broad Grand Union Locks have given way to narrow, just wide enough to take a single narrow boat. Past the second lock a railway bridge, painted in blue, is followed by a busy road interchange. The canal sweeps round to the left under a new road bridge with the image of a working boat picked out in brick on the wall. The locks continue on down to Bordesley Junction, where the canal divides: the old Birmingham and Warwick going off to the right and the Digbeth Branch, which the path follows, going to Birmingham on the left. This is the original Warwick and Birmingham line. Cross the typical Birmingham iron bridge, its parapet wall grooved by tow ropes, and turn left.

You now enter an area of old canal-oriented factories, broken by a two-arched aqueduct over a culverted river. The view offers a wide range of architecture, from the classical portico of the old Curzon Street station to the telecommunications tower and the modern office blocks. Once through the next railway bridge, follow the path round to the right to a tunnel-like passage under a complex of rails. A delicately incised bollard at the far end marks the arrival of the six Ashted Locks and the start of the final climb to the city centre. This is a very enclosed world, in the city but separate from it, typified by the canal house by Belmont Road Bridge, with its neat garden and miniature watermill. Isolation is increased by a walk through the dark, low and rather creepy Ashted Tunnel, which leads to an area of brand-new development. The buildings use the latest hi-tech styles, but the developers have very much made the canal part of the whole scheme, restoring bridges and towpath. Old and new meet happily here: the bronzed glass of a tower block reflects the ornate ironwork of huge gas-holders.

At the next, or Aston, junction, marked by the crisp black and white iron bridge, turn left and head for the cluster of towers that marks the city centre. Some may not like this almost aggressively urban environment, but no one can deny its drama. The canal climbs steeply up the thirteen locks of the Farmers Bridge flight. At Snow Hill the railway viaduct crosses on a long row of arches; old warehouses have loading bays and canopies, while a modern concrete block strides right across a lock on concrete stilts – and there are memories of Birmingham's industrial past in the shape of the steam engines that can be glimpsed in the Industrial Museum. Cambrian Wharf at the top of the flight was one of the first of Birmingham's canal-side areas to be developed as an amenity, with old buildings refurbished and a new pub added. Now it is overshadowed by the National Indoor Arena **(C)**. Turn left over the iron bridge at Farmers Bridge Junction for the last stage to Gas Street Basin. Not many years ago this was a hidden area of Birmingham, surrounded by old warehouses: now there is another new pub, looking out on a colourful array of old working boats, and it is surrounded by the vast complex of hotels and the International Convention Centre. The walk that began in central London has finally arrived in the very heart of Birmingham.

A38(M)

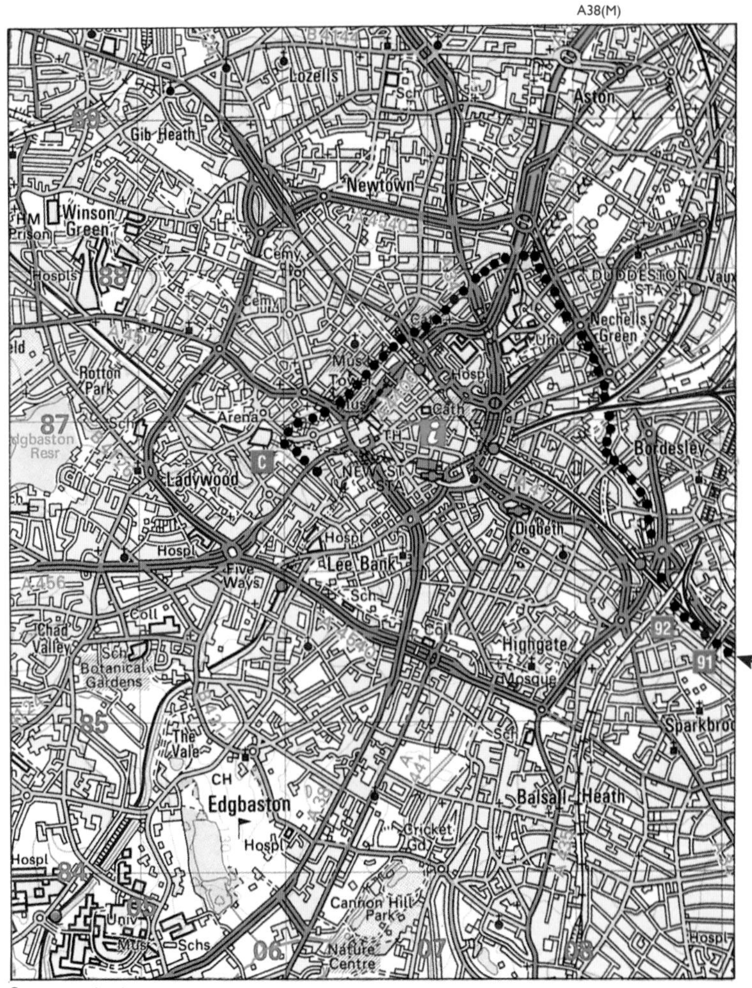

Contours are given in metres
The vertical interval is 10m

The city begins to crowd in at Camp Hill locks, yet still the path retains its

border of green.

The communication tower stands as an exclamation mark, announcing journey's end in the centre of Birmingham.

PART THREE
Useful Information

Transport

There is good regular public transport along the Grand Union route throughout the year. The most remote place on the canal is barely 2 miles (3 km) from the nearest bus service. Some important services are provided by smaller bus operators and other key points only show up regularly on express coach services. However the greatest asset of the route for most of its length is the very close proximity of rail services, notably between Watford and Northampton, and between Leamington Spa and Birmingham.

Rail

London Transport

The Metropolitan line serves Uxbridge, Rickmansworth and Watford.

The Piccadilly line serves Uxbridge and Alperton.

British Rail

The Euston–Rugby line serves Kings's Langley, Apsley, Hemel Hempstead, Berkhamsted, Tring, Leighton Buzzard and Milton Keynes.

The Aylesbury–Marylebone line serves Rickmansworth.

The Paddington–Reading line serves Acton, Hanwell, Southall, Hayes & Harlington, West Drayton and Iver.

Brentford is on line to Waterloo.

The Leamington Spa to Birmingham Snowhill line serves Hatton, Lapworth, Solihull, Olton, Acocks Green, Tyseley and Bordesley.

Buses

Long-distance coach services link with the Grand Union at many points throughout the route, including all the principal towns and the major trunk routes.

Contacts

National Express, London	071 730 0202
London, Victoria Coach Station	071 730 3466
South Midlands (Oxford)	0865 791579
East Midlands (Peterborough)	0733 237141
Birmingham	021 622 4372

Regional and local bus services provide an extensive network of transport throughout the Grand Union route. All services within London are coordinated by London Transport and in the West Midlands by Centro. The five county councils *en route* also coordinate local public transport and often produce combined timetables at modest cost.

ACCOMMODATION

British Waterways have produced a useful booklet to help you find accommodation along the Grand Union Canal Walk. This is available from British Waterways, The Stop House, Braunston, Northants NN11 7JQ. Tel: 0788 890666.

Tourist boards can give advice on accommodation and some have produced leaflets. There are youth hostels at Badby, Birmingham, Milton Keynes and Ivinghoe and in London.

Tourist Information Centres

These are useful for advice about local services and can usually book accommodation in advance.

Centres open all year are to be found at:

Aylesbury: County Hall, Walton Street, Aylesbury, Bucks HP20 1UA. Tel: 0296 382308/383095

Berkhamsted: The Library, Kings Road, Berkhamsted, Herts HP4 3BD. Tel: 0442 877638

Birmingham: Convention and Visitor Bureau, 2 City Arcade, Birmingham, West Midlands B2 4TX. Tel: 021 643 2514

Daventry: Moot Hall, Market Square, Daventry, Northants NN11 4BH. Tel: 0327 300277

Hemel Hempstead: Pavilion Box Office, Marlowes, Hemel Hempstead, Herts HP1 1HA. Tel: 0442 64451

Leamington Spa: Jephson Lodge, Jephson Gardens, The Parade, Leamington Spa, Warwickshire CV32 4AB. Tel: 0926 311470

Milton Keynes: 536 Silbury Boulevard, Milton Keynes, Bucks MK9 3AF. Tel: 0908 232525

Northampton: Visitor Centre, Mr Grants House, 10 St Giles Square, Northampton NN1 1DA. Tel: 0604 22677

Rickmansworth: Three Rivers House, Northway, Rickmansworth, Herts WD3 1RL. Tel: 0923 776611 ext. 1381

Solihull: Central Library, Homer Road, West Midlands B91 3RG. Tel: 021 704 6130/6134

Warwick: The Court House, Jury Street, Warwick, Warwickshire CV34 4EW. Tel: 0926 492212
Wendover: The Clock Tower, Wendover, Bucks HP22 6DU. Tel: 0296 623056

For regional information, contact the following tourist boards:
London Tourist Board, 26 Grosvenor Gardens, London SW1 0DU. Tel: 071 730 3488
Heart of England Tourist Board, Woodside, Larkhill, Worcester WR5 2EF. Tel: 0905 763436
East Midlands Tourist Board, Exchequergate, Lincoln LN2 1PZ. Tel: 0522 531521

USEFUL ADDRESSES

Backpackers Club, 20 St Michael's Road, Tilehurst, Reading RG3 4RP.
Berks, Bucks & Oxon Naturalists' Trust (BBONT), Dr Rachel Thomas, Haydon Mill, Rabans Lane, Aylesbury HP19 3ST.
Birmingham Canal Navigations Society, Secretary: 9 Firbank Way, Pelsall, Walsall, West Midlands. Tel: 0922 682931.
British Trust for Ornithology, Beech Grove, Tring, Herts HP23 5NR.

British Waterways
British Waterways, Willow Grange, Church Road, Watford, Herts WD1 3QA.
Waterway Offices:
Little Venice 071 286 6101
Marsworth 044 282 5938
Hatton 0926 492192
Braunston 0788 890666
South East Regional Office: Brindley House, Corner Hall, Lawn Lane, Hemel Hempstead, Herts HP3 9YT. Tel: 0442 235400.
Midlands Regional Office: Peels Wharf, Lichfield Street, Fazeley, Staffs B78 3QZ. Tel: 0827 252000.

Colne Valley Park Groundwork Trust, Denham Court, Village Road, Denham UB95 5BG. Tel: 0895 832662.
Cyclists Touring Club, 69 Meadrow, Godalming, Surrey GU7 3HS.
English Nature (formerly the Nature Conservancy Council), Northminster House, Peterborough PE1 1UA. Tel: 0733 340345.

Grand Union Canal Society, Ian Wilson, 13 Dacre Close, Millet Road, Greenford, Middx UB6 9UQ.

Herts & Middlesex Wildlife Trust, Grebe House, St Michael's Street, St Albans, Herts AL3 4SN. Tel: 0727 58901/54502.

Inland Waterways Association, 114 Regent's Park Road, London NW1 8UQ. Tel: 071 586 2556/2510.

Long Distance Walkers' Association, 29 Appledown Road, Alresford, Hampshire SO24 2DN.

National Off-road Bicycle Association, 139 Tooley Street, London SE1 2NZ.

National Trust

London Office: 36 Queen Anne's Gate, London SW1H 9AS. Tel: 071 222 9251.

East Midlands: Clumber Park Stableyard, Worksop, Notts S80 3BE. Tel: 0909 702021.

Severn: Mythe End House, Tewkesbury, Glos GL20 6EB. Tel: 0684 850051.

Southern: Polesden Lacey, Dorking, Surrey RH5 6BD. Tel: 0372 453401.

Thames & Chilterns: Hughenden Manor, High Wycombe, Bucks HP14 4LA. Tel: 0494 528051.

Northamptonshire Countryside Centre, 9 Guildhall Road, Northampton. Tel: 0604 237220.

The Open Spaces Society, 25a Bell Street, Henley-on-Thames, Oxon RG9 2BA.

Ordnance Survey, Romsey Road, Maybush, Southampton SO9 4DH.

Ramblers Association, 1–5 Wandsworth Road, London SW8 2XX.

Royal Society for the Protection of Birds, The Lodge, Sandy, Beds SG19 2DL.

Youth Hostels Association, Trevelyan House, 8 St Stephen's Hill, St Albans, Herts AL1 2DT.

Places to Visit

Little Venice

Cascade Floating Gallery. Tel: 071 289 7050

Rickmansworth

Canal Centre, Batchworth Locks.

Three Rivers Museum, Basing House, 46 High Street, Rickmansworth.
Moor Park Mansion (one mile south east of Rickmansworth). Tel: 0923 773146.

Watford

Watford Museum, 194 High Street, Watford. Tel: 0923 32297.

Berkhamsted

Berkhamsted Castle. Tel: 0442 862411. Map reference SP 996083).

Tring

British Trust for Ornithology, Tring. Tring Reservoirs.
The Ashridge Estate (National Trust), Ivinghoe Hills. Estate open all year. Shop and information centre.
Zoological Museum, Akeman Street, Tring. Tel: 044282 4181. Map reference SP 941166.

Ivinghoe

Ford End Watermill, Ivinghoe (600 yards north of Ivinghoe church.) Tel: 0582 600391.
Pitstone Windmill, Ivinghoe (1/2 mile south of Ivinghoe, map reference SP 946158).

Pitstone Green

Pitstone Green Farm Museum. Tel: 0296 661997.

Leighton Buzzard

Leighton Buzzard Railway, Pages Park Station, Billington Road, Leighton Buzzard. Tel: 0525 373888. On A4146, map reference SP 928242.

Great Linford

Arc Wildfowl Centre, Great Linford Pits. Tel: 0908 604820.

Milton Keynes

Milton Keynes Museum of Industry and Rural Life, Stacey Hill Farm, Southern Way, Wolverton. Tel: 0908 319148/316222. Access off MK Grid Road H2, Millers Way or off Southern Way.

Bradwell

Bradwell Windmill, off Grafton Street, Bradville. Tel: 0908 678361.

Stoke Park

Stoke Park Pavilions. Tel: 0604 862172.

Stoke Bruerne

Canal Museum. Tel: 0604 862229.

Upper Stowe

Old Dairy Farm Craft Centre, Upper Stowe. Tel: 0327 40525.

Warwick

The Court House, Jury Street. Tel: 0926 492212.

Warwick Doll Museum, Oken's House. Tel: 0926 495546 or 410410 ext 2500.
Lord Leycester Hospital, High Street. Tel: 0926 492797.
St Johns House, St Johns. Tel: 0926 410410 ext 2021.
Warwick Castle, off Castle Hill. Tel: 0926 495421.
Warwickshire Museum, Market Place. Tel: 0926 412500/412501.
Warwickshire Yeomanry Museum, The Court House Vaults, Jury Street. Tel: 0926 492212.

Hatton

Country World, Dark Lane, Hatton. Tel: 0926 842436.

Baddesley Clinton

Baddesley Clinton House (National Trust). Tel: 0564 783294. Map reference SP 199723.

Lapworth

Packwood House (National Trust). Tel: 0564 782024. Map reference SP 174722.

Knowle

Chester House, Knowle Library, 1667–9 High Street, Knowle. Tel: 0564 775840.

Bickenhill

National Motorcycle Museum, Bickenhill. Tel: 06756 3311. Map reference SP 199828.

Birmingham

Birmingham Railway Museum, 670 Warwick Road, Tyseley. Tel: 021 707 4696.
Museum of Science and Industry, Newhall Street. Tel: 021 236 1022.
Birmingham Museum and Art Gallery, Chamberlain Square. Tel: 021 235 2834.
Birmingham Cathedral, Colmore Row.
Birmingham Jewellery Quarter. Tel: 021 643 2514.

Aylesbury Arm

Wilstone

Wilstone Reservoir, National Nature Reserve.

Aylesbury

Buckinghamshire County Museum, St Marys Square, Church Street, Aylesbury. Tel: 0296 88849.

Brentford Arm

Isleworth

Osterley Park and House, map reference TQ 146780. Access

from Thornbury Road north of A4 ¼ mile east of Osterley station. Tel: 081 560 3918.

Brentford

Boston Manor House, Boston Manor Road, Brentford. Tel: 081 862 5805.

The Musical Museum, 368 High Street, Brentford. Tel: 081 560 8108.

Kew Bridge Steam Museum, The Pumping Station, Green Dragon Lane. Tel: 081 568 4757.

Syon House and Syon Park Gardens, on north bank of River Thames between Brentford and Isleworth.
Tel: 081 560 0881/3.

Royal Botanic Gardens at Kew. Tel: 081 940 1171.

Northampton Arm

Hunsbury Hill

Hunsbury Hill Ironstone Railway, Industrial Museum and Country Park, Hunsbury Hill Road, Camp Hill.
Tel: 085 889 216.

Delapre Park and Gardens with Delapre Abbey.

Northampton

Museum of Leathercraft, The Old Blue Coat School, Bridge Street. Tel: 0604 39415.

Central Museum and Art Gallery, Guildhall Road.
Tel: 0604 39415.

Carlsberg Brewery Ltd, Bridge Street, Northampton.
Tel: 0604 234433.

Guildhall, St Giles Square, Northampton. Tel: 0604 34881.

GUIDED WALKS

Many of the county councils through which the Grand Union Canal Walk passes organize guided walks programmes, often throughout the year. Some of these walks include sections of the canal.

Contacts:
Hertfordshire Countryside Management Service,
County Information Officer,
Planning & Estates,
County Hall,
Hertford
Tel: 0992 555257

Buckingham County Council,
County Surveyors Office,
County Offices,
Aylesbury, Bucks
Tel: 0296 395000

Northamptonshire Countryside Centre,
9 Guildhall Road,
Northampton
Tel: 0604 237227

There are also programmes organised by local ramblers groups.

British Waterways have in recent years provided a summer series of canal and reservoir walks in Northamptonshire. Contact 0788 890666.

The Inland Waterways Association runs a full programme of canal-side walks in London: IWA, 114 Regents Park Road, London NW1 8UQ. Tel: 071 586 2556/2510.

TRIP BOATS

There are no scheduled public services by boat along the Grand Union. However, a number of local trip boat operators do have regular departures on short excursions during the summer months. Telephone each operator for details:

Camden – Little Venice
London Waterbus Co. 071 482 2550
Jason's Trip 071 286 3428
Jenny Wren Cruises 071 485 4433/6210
Uxbridge
Colne Valley Passenger Boat Services 0895 812130 081 571 4428
Watford
Arcturus Cruises 043871 4528
Marsworth–Tring
Grebe Canal Cruises 0296 661920
Leighton Buzzard
Leighton Lady Cruises 0525 384563
Stoke Bruerne
Linda Cruises 0604 862107
Indian Chief 0604 862428
Birmingham Gas Street
Birmingham and Midland Canal Carrying 021 643 0525
Brummagem Boats 021 455 6163

ANGLING ON THE GRAND UNION CANAL

In his book, *The Complete Coarse Fisherman* (Ward Lock, 1987), the well-known angler, publisher and broadcaster, David Hall, has written '. . . canals have been the training ground for many of today's top anglers' and 'The secret . . . is to think small.' But, although canals are no longer the working highways they once were, they still carry a good deal of boat traffic, so the first step for any angler is to locate the lie of the fish, usually on shelves untroubled by the churning of pleasure cruisers and narrow boats.

Throughout its length from London to Birmingham, the Grand Union Canal offers varied and interesting fishing opportunities. The most important species in the Grand Union is the roach. In the canal, roach average between 1 ounce and 8 ounces (compare that with record-breaking fish of over 4 pounds), although fish in excess of 1 pound have been taken. On some stretches of the canal, there are many shoals of bream, with specimens weighing up to 5 pounds. The Grand Union also holds a surprisingly good stock of perch and occasionally fish of more than 3 pounds have been caught; the Milton Keynes–Braunston stretch of the canal is particularly noted for its specimen fish. Chub of up to 5 pounds in weight are plentiful on those canal sections that connect with rivers – the Cassiobury Park pound at Watford, for example. Carp have been stocked in some sections of the canal and grow well, reaching more than 20 pounds in weight. The Watford–Milton Keynes section is worthy of special mention for specimen carp. Because the heavy boat traffic colours the water, pike – which hunt by sight – are not able to grow to a particularly large size in the canal although fish of over 10 pounds have been reported.

Generally, it is more difficult to catch canal fish than their counterparts in a lake or river, and to become a competent canal angler requires no little skill. Many casual anglers make the mistake of using line that is much too heavy, hooks that are much too large, and bait that is inappropriate for the likely size of the fish. Canal experts usually use poles, with their associated end tackle, for match fishing. For the casual angler, however, an old-fashioned rod and reel approach is just as good. Start off with a line strength of 2 to 3 pounds, a hook size 20 or 22, and a single maggot or pinkie as bait. About one pint of bait should be enough for a four- or five-hour fishing session. Groundbait, if used at all, should be introduced on a little-but-often basis because the regular movement of boats soon carries it away from the fishing area. It is important to introduce feed regularly.

The fishing rights on the Grand Union Canal are let by British Waterways to various angling clubs and associations. Most clubs allow anglers to fish the canal on a day-permit basis. The typical cost of a day permit at the time of writing is about £1.50–£3.00. There are a few clubs that actually reserve sections for club members only, so before you start fishing please read any angling club notices that you might see. These should tell you whether or not day permits are available. In addition to a permit, all anglers must, by law, possess a National Rivers Authority Rod Licence. These are available from most good fishing tackle shops.

You can get more information about canal fishing from:

Regional Fisheries Manager
British Waterways
Brindley House
Corner Hall
Lawn Lane
Hemel Hempstead
Herts
HP3 9YT

BIBLIOGRAPHY

David Blagrove, *Bread Upon the Waters*, Pearsons, 1984
—*Waterways of Northamptonshire*, 1990
British Waterways, *Through London by Canal 1885*, 1977
Anthony Burton, *Canal Mania*, Aurum Press, 1993
Bob & Elizabeth Bush, *The Aylesbury and Wendover Canals*, ACS, 1988
Chris Cove-Smith, *London's Waterways Guide*, ILN & W, 1977
Neil Curtis, *The Ridgeway, National Trail Guide*, Aurum Press, 1989
Martyn Denney, *Historic Waterways Scenes, London and South East England*, Moorland, 1980
—*London's Waterways*, Batsford, 1977
Geoff Elwin & Cathleen King, *The Stratford upon Avon and Warwick Canals*, Blackthorn, 1980
—*Braunston to Brentford*, Blackthorn, 1980
—*The Grand Union Canal from the Chilterns to the Thames*, Blackthorn, 1981
Alan Faulkner, *The Grand Junction Canal*, David & Charles, 1972
—*The Willow Wren Story*, Waterway Productions, 1986

Graham Greene, *A Sort of Life*, Bodley Head, 1971
Charles Hadfield, *The Canals of the East Midlands*, David & Charles, 1970
Charles Hadfield & A. W. Skempton, *William Jessop, Engineer*, David & Charles, 1979
John Hassell, *A Tour of the Grand Junction Canal in 1819*, Cranfield & Bonfield, 1968
Derek Pratt, *Southern Inland Waterways*, Ian Allan, 1982

Ordnance Survey Maps Covering The Walk

Landranger Maps (scale: 1:50,000) 139, 151, 152, 165, 166, 176
Pathfinder Maps (scale: 1:25,000)

934	SP 08/18	1023	SP 64/74	1139	TQ 09/19
954	SP 07/17	1024	SP 84/94	1158	TQ 08/18
975	SP 06/16	1047	SP 83/93	1174	TQ 07/17
976	SP 26/36	1071	SP 82/92	1175	TQ 27/37
977	SP 46/56	1094	SP 81/91	1157	SU 88/98
978	SP 66/76	1118	SP 80/90		
1000	SP 65/75	1119	TL 00/10		

The Grand Union Canal and the National Network

The main line of the Grand Union is the longest single canal in Britain. But its 140 miles represent only 7 per cent of the whole 2,000 miles of waterway managed by British Waterways for the benefit of the public.

British Waterways has looked after the nationalized canals and river navigations for thirty years. In that time leisure and tourism have emerged as the dominant functions of the network, though freight transport, drainage and water transfer remain important on particular routes.

The overall aim of British Waterways is to conserve the environment and heritage of this 200-year-old monument to civil engineering, architecture, commercial enterprise and social change. By any standard it is a unique inheritance for us all.

Stewardship of the inland waterways involves opening them up so that we can all appreciate their value. It also requires the generation, where appropriate, of revenue for waterway maintenance and development so that a viable asset is passed on to future generations. In round terms, the network costs £80 million a year to run. It is funded partly by income from rents, leases, tolls, licences and profits from subsidiary businesses. The remainder is received from central government in the form of annual grant aid.

Around ten million people use the canals every year for leisure. They boat, fish on the water and cycle, run, walk, paint or photograph along the towpath. To avoid potential conflicts of interest, British Waterways, in working to a charter for waterway users, has developed policies which aim to make the most of canals.

Safety is of paramount importance. British Waterways also lays emphasis on high standards of facilities and service, and encourages courtesy among waterway users. Opportunities for earning income from the tourism potential of the canals are pursued within the context of conserving the canal environment and heritage.

These national policies are translated into action by local management units grouped in regions. Around twenty local managers are the first point of contact for waterway users; details of those covering the Grand Union are listed under Useful Addresses at the end of this guide. Each manager's stretch of waterway is maintained to standards agreed with local representative groups – standards which include the condition of towpaths.

On the subject of towpath maintenance, tribute should be paid to the extensive improvements to towpaths and their access points by bodies other than British Waterways. Many local authorities, park authorities, public trusts, businesses and voluntary societies have funded and carried out work with British Waterways which has dramatically extended leisure opportunities for us all, on foot, on cycles or in wheelchairs. For instance, the whole concept of the Grand Union Canal Walk has involved contributions from nearly every borough, district and county council on the route.

Having all indirectly paid for the public funding of our waterways through national and local taxes, we should make good use of them. And there is no better time than the present.

During 1993 and 1994 canals all over the country are celebrating their bicentenaries. British Waterways has coordinated a host of events, shows and exhibitions under the 'Canals 200' banner. 1793 was the height of canal mania when 62 canals, half the system, were being planned, promoted or built. Three constituent companies of the Grand Union were among them and the launch of the Grand Union Canal Walk in July 1993 is a fitting commemoration of the vision which those eighteenth-century financiers, politicians, civil engineers and navvies turned into reality.

Key to 1:50 000 scale main mapping (selected items)
Approx. 1 1/4 inches to 1 mile

ROADS AND PATHS
Not necessarily rights of way

Labels on symbol	Meaning
Service area; M 1; Elevated; 1 Junction number	Motorway (dual carriageway)
Unfenced; A 40 (T); Footbridge	Trunk road
A 438; Dual carriageway	Main road
	Main road under construction
B 4348	Secondary road
Bridge	Road generally more than 4m wide
	Road generally less than 4m wide
	Other road, drive or track
	Path

RAILWAYS

- Track multiple or single
- Station, principal
- Bridges, Footbridge
- Tunnel
- Embankment, cutting
- Viaduct

WATER FEATURES

- Canal, lock
- Canal (dry)
- Aqueduct
- Footbridge

Key to 1:25 000 scale circular walk mapping (selected items)
Approx. 2 1/2 inches to 1 mile

ROADS AND PATHS
Not necessarily rights of way

Labels on symbol	Meaning
M1 or A6(M)	Motorway
A 31(T)	Trunk or Main road
B 3074	Secondary road
A 35	Dual carriageway
	Road generally more than 4m wide
	Road generally less than 4m wide
	Other road, drive or track

Unfenced roads and tracks are shown by pecked lines

- Path

RAILWAYS

- Multiple track } Standard gauge
- Single track } Standard gauge
- Tunnel; cutting; embankment
- Road over; road under; level crossing

PUBLIC RIGHTS OF WAY

Public rights of way shown on this map may not be evident on the ground

- Public paths: Footpath, Bridleway
- Byway open to all traffic
- Road used as a public path

The representation on this map of any other road, track or path is no evidence of the existence of a right of way

---

Canal walk symbols

- Route of walk
- A Feature reference point
- 95 Bridge number
- Hazard
- Start of circular walk
- Direction of circular walk
- Ancient monument
- Information centre
- Caravan site
- Picnic site